ANDRÉ LE NÔTRE

ANDRÉ LE NÔTRE

GARDENER TO THE SUN KING

*

ÉRIK ORSENNA

Translated from the French by

MOISHE BLACK

GEORGE BRAZILLER * NEW YORK

The translator gratefully acknowledges the help of typist Kathleen Swann, technical expert Ronald Kachur, and mathematician Garth Thomas.

Originally published in France by Librairie Arthème Fayard in 2000 under the title *Portrait d'un homme heureux: André Le Nôtre, 1613–1700*

First published in the United States of America by George Braziller, Inc., in 2001

For information, please address the publisher:
George Braziller, Inc.
171 Madison Avenue
New York, NY 10016

Library of Congress Cataloging-in-Publication Data:

Orsenna, Erik, 1947-
   [Portrait d'un homme heureux. English]
   André Le Nôtre: gardener to the sun king/Érik Orsenna; translated from the French by
   Moishe Black.
      p. cm.
   Includes bibliographical references (p.).
   ISBN 0-8076-1487-4 (hc)
   1. Le Nâtre, Andrâ, 1613-1700. 2. Landscape architects–France–Biography. 3. Gardens,
French–History–17th century. 4. Gardens–France–Design–History–17th century. I. Title.

SB470.L4 07713 2001
712'.092–dc21
[B]   2001025617

Design by Christopher Moisan

Printed and bound in the United States of America

First edition

For my mother

CONTENTS

"You are a happy man, Le Nôtre."

—Louis XIV

I.

THE GEOGRAPHY FAIRIES

An exhausted midwife, smelling so strongly of sweat and blood that she was followed by a whole cohort of cats, was plodding home to her abode on the rue Saint-Nicaise. At that moment in time, the Japanese were slowly digesting their humiliating defeat at the hands of the Koreans. In India the Mughals reigned. Moscow had just driven out the Poles, and the first of the Romanovs was the new tsar. On the shores of the Bosporus, the goings-on of Mehmed III had recently caused a certain degree of concern: it was generally felt that to have his nineteen brothers and some score of his sisters strangled by deaf-mutes on the very day he acceded to the throne was going too far. As a result it was decided that power would be entrusted to the sultanas. Farther west, Ragusa was casting envious eyes on Venice. In the newly created town of Santa Fe, New Mexico, the Franciscan monks were baptizing Pueblo, Hopi Mesa, Cuarac, and Tajique Indians by the thousands, and on holy days the inhabitants vied with one another to see who could find the cruelest form of self-flagellation. In Brazil, meanwhile, around São Paulo (a town of three thousand souls), the Jesuits harried and hunted down those increasingly numerous Portuguese immigrants who were finding heathen life in the jungle and the charms of native women more to their taste than the benefits of civilization.

As for France, the wealthiest country in Europe had long been wasted by a major scourge, civil war. The French slit each other's throats for fun and called it religious dispute. King Louis XIII was only twelve years old. His mother, Marie de Médicis, kept the regency going as best she could, paying the Great Nobles not to make trouble, which meant that one-fifth of the budget disappeared into the clutches of greedy fingers already weighted down with precious rings. Not a single frontier was secure. The Spaniards had possession of le Nord and Artois, of Franche-Comté and Roussillon. The Empire controlled Alsace and Lorraine. Nice and Savoy were foreign territory as well . . .

Under Henri IV, the French grew peaceable; thanks to Sully, they grew rich. Skies were calm, until Ravaillac's knife brought back the storms. Sixteen thirteen was no different from the difficult years preceding it: days, like waves, to be breasted one at a time and quickly forgotten so you would have courage enough to live through the next, and the one after. In this heavily charged atmosphere, who, except his parents, could attach any importance at all to the birth of André, son of John, himself the son of Pierre, both of them gardeners?

* * *

Only the geography fairies, their heads bowed attentively over a map of Paris, found cause for wonderment. These good ladies thought, not without reason, that the place where you are born determines your fate. The genius, that is, the guiding spirit, of a place carries far more weight than all that zodiac rubbish.

Consider (said the fairies) where the house of his birth is located. To begin with, almost on its doorstep is a royal palace, the Louvre, seat of all the powers that be. To move with practiced ease among the great and mighty requires long apprenticeship, which the close proximity of a palace cannot fail to provide. Breathing the same air they breathe will help the child read their moods.

The fairies' eyes glisten. There are attractive career possibilities here; quick, let's see what else we can find.

Other immediate neighbors are the Feuillants Monastery and the Royal Riding Academy. As background music to your start in life, what could be better than human prayers mingling with horses' hoofbeats, one lifting you up toward the clouds while the other calls you back to earth? To the north, Quinze-Vingts, home for the blind, a constant reminder of sight and its importance. Lastly, just outside young André's door, the gardens, an inexhaustible dictionary for the little lad to consult, as soon as his legs can take him out of the house.

In short, this child had been born in the right place for rising to great heights while keeping both feet on the ground.

Rapt in contemplation of their nursling, the parents had not heard any of these cogitations. Nothing remained for the fairies but to take their leave and follow the midwife. I can imagine them on the dark staircase, their robes getting tangled as they made their way down, vexed at not having roused greater interest, when what they had to offer were the only truths that count, truths that mature slowly. Their frustration will come as no surprise: such disappointments are the daily lot of anyone, man or woman, who is partial to geography.

II.

A Bit of Tuscany

T he story of the Tuileries had begun sixty years earlier.[1]
Haunted by the memory of her husband, Henri II, who
had been killed while jousting near the rue Saint-Antoine, Catherine
de Médicis had taken a dislike to the Louvre. It was too old, too
gray, and too sad. Five hundred and fifty yards farther west, at right
angles to the Seine, she had had a palace built for her use. And more
to the point, a palace with grounds. She was a true Italian, and what
she had missed these many years was gardens, in particular the
Boboli Gardens where she had spent her childhood before coming
to live in dark and gloomy France.

The place was nothing special: a patch of uncultivated land at the
water's edge, a hundred acres of woodland and thickets. Tilers lived
there, for the sake of the red clay along the riverbanks. They were
requested to go and ply their trade elsewhere. A Florentine was
hired, Bernard de Carnessequi, and was immediately named *intendant des plantes*. Three French gardeners came to assist him, including a certain Pierre Le Nostre. They laid out paths bordered with
sycamores, elms, and firs. They planted flowers and all sorts of food-
bearing species, large and small. Soon, rising out of the soil, there
were orchards and vegetable gardens, pear trees and cherries, orange

trees and almonds. A bit of Tuscany under the skies of Île-de-France.

Completing the illusion, the builders added a great number of fountains; they designed a labyrinth of willows and furnished it with benches that would greatly shock the Swiss ambassadors, quick to guess at the "bad things" people could get up to in these secluded spots. The renowned Bernard Palissy was pressed into service; he built a "rustic grotto" with mosaics covering its walls.

Queen Catherine had begun to enjoy life again. Court life was a succession of fêtes, some private, others diplomatic. In September of 1573, she received the Polish plenipotentiaries who had come to offer their country's throne to her son Henri. In a salon of greenery, a ballet, "the finest ever seen," was presented for their entertainment. Among its many surprise effects was an enormous rock that suddenly began to move, carrying along the hundred musicians who stood upon it.

Nor were ordinary Parisians neglected. To help the people forget their woes, festivities intended specially for them were held regularly at the Tuileries, and everyone came away with a head full of dazzling memories.

Henri IV, called le Béarnais, kept up the Florentine tradition. Like his mother, his wife was a Medici by birth. But long before he married, he had grasped the fact that his French kingdom's foremost source of wealth was its land. He had read Olivier de Serres's treatise *Théâtre d'agriculture et mesnage des champs* and been convinced. On numerous occasions he received at court the author of this treatise on field husbandry. They would walk for hours side by side, conversing and deciding which farming methods were the best. The king developed a passion for his gardens. Prospects in the Tuileries were given more breathing space, the paths were broadened, and water flowed abundantly, thanks to the Samaritaine. This was a pump invented by Flemish engineer Jean Lintlaër; he had set it up on a piling of the Pont-Neuf, itself just barely completed.

To the ornamental was added the useful, even the industrial. We're buying silk from our neighbors, are we? Can't tolerate that sort of dependence! Henri IV decided to plant twenty thousand mulberry trees in the Tuileries. A specialist from Italy, Giulia by name, lovingly mothered her silkworms in the newly built orangery.

In all these developments the Le Nostres were involved, whether as spectators or participants: Jean worked with his father on the flower beds until a day came when the responsibility was his alone. By the time André appeared on the scene, the stage was already set: a garden constantly being embellished to please princes, astonish the populace, and enhance the nation's prestige.

III

ISLAND AMID THE FRENZIED FEVERS

M orning. Out there, at the end of a longish avenue carrying you back in time, two silhouettes. A child runs and skips around the legs of a man. The man is talking. It's garden-lesson time. Birds are singing. A dog is digging hopefully at the ground. A father is taking his son for a walk in the world of plants. He's teaching the child to recognize plants and put names to them, to look at them and smell them. He's teaching him how bees are useful, that Comice pears eaten too green give you colic, how the seasons move and change, that you have to work the soil in winter if you want an abundant spring. The little lad plays with the dog and acts as though he were hearing not one word. Who cares about the official school, the one he attends? For your first teacher, a papa who knows about the natural world; what more could a child ask?

There was no end to what the Tuileries could offer. Animals abounded. A gentleman had even been appointed "governor of wild beasts," a title of distinction showing that he was responsible for the menagerie where lions and tigers could be heard to roar, accompanied by bears and wolves. But the greatest space of all had been set aside for horses: a long racecourse, where king and lords came to hone their skills at games that were in fashion. For example, tilting at the ring: like today's youngsters on their carousel steeds, the horsemen had to gallop at full tilt and try to spear a hanging iron loop with the point of their lances. One can imagine young André clapping his hands as he watched these royal exercises.

The finer points displayed at the Royal Stables, a little farther east, were beyond him. Horseback riding was much more than a means of transport: it was cultivated as one of the fine arts. A riding academy had been started up; besides equestrian science, it taught geometry and music. Knowledge of the horse was, in that era, one of the core elements of civilization. A century later, François Robichon de la Guérinière would publish what amounted to a code of horsemanship, still considered authoritative today.

The remainder of the Tuileries domain was devoted to hunting, another passion among men of noble birth. Louis XIII learned the rudiments of this pursuit while still very young. He was taught how to set his horse at wild boars or roebucks or even wildcats. Did the Le Nostre family witness a scene that made the child king weep? His favorite dogs had been torn to shreds by a lion. His attention was quickly diverted to gentler pursuits, crossbow archery or the training of falcons.

* *
 *

These cruel rustic pastimes were as courtly gallantries compared to the acts of violence that tore Paris limb from limb with depressing regularity. Protected by moats and high walls, the enclave formed by the Tuileries was an island floating serenely amid the frenzied fevers of the city. To step outside those walls was to set foot in the battle zone. From the Saint Bartholomew's Day Massacre of 1572 until the final furies of the Fronde in 1653, not a year went by without the Le Nostres hearing the clash of arms as they prudently took shelter in their house, which was too well situated, too close to the palaces. The pretext for these combats changed; the reasons given might be now feudal, now religious, but the true motive remained constant: the struggle for power. And civil war never stopped; the French went right on tearing each other's guts out. It was only natural that the worst confrontations should be hosted by the kingdom's capital city. Parisians would not soon forget the cries and hoofbeats of a certain August night, nor the visions of horror revealed by dawning day, thousands of Protestant corpses, nobleman and shopkeeper alike, strewn in the streets or floating belly up along the Seine as though to mock the heavens. That day their river ran red. Nor had the people of Paris forgotten how Henri IV besieged their city, the repeated assaults of his armies, and the terror prevailing within its walls on account of the Holy League. And the gnawing hunger.

In 1610, Ravaillac's regicidal folly lit the fires once again. Young André had but to lend an ear or, ignoring his parents' strict prohibitions, glance stealthily out between the closed shutters. He was growing up surrounded by the sights and sounds of anarchy. Duels, brawls, riots . . . such was the daily portion served up beneath his windows. Louis XIII, at the age of fifteen and a half, was about to offer him better fare: there at the Louvre, which is to say just a few yards away, this adolescent king suddenly gave orders for the assassination of Concini, his mother's favorite. Three volleys of pistol shots and that was the end of this greedy, tyrannical, universally detested maréchal. Word of his death was hailed by the populace, and celebrations went on all night long. At the Church of Saint-Germain-l'Auxerrois, a mob detected the freshly dug grave, disinterred the corpse, carved it up, and fought over the pieces, some of which they hung up while others they cooked . . . Perhaps, in the mind of a very small boy (André, age four), a feeling, rather like a penchant for order and moderation, was awakened that day.

Indeed, between these fits of madness, daily life in the city was a rather unappetizing affair that would make anyone long for a bit of order. Getting from one place to another, even a place very near by, took on the flavor of adventure. A tortuous tracery of buildings, alleyways so constricted that two carriages could not pass, a mania for corbels blocking every possible view of the sky, the unending creak of low-hanging signboards for you to whack your skull on, muddy, often stopped-up gutters down the middle of the streets, accumulations of refuse still there in spite of ordinances, a rats' paradise and breeding ground for epidemics, highwaymen by the score, and other ruffians whose ways were more fearful still . . . Such was the most populous city in Christendom (three hundred thousand souls), its praises sung by every admiring visitor!

The Le Nostre family home had its back turned to Paris and its face to the Tuileries, clearly a situation big with symbolism and bound to bring forth a vocation. Gardens were destined to repay a hundredfold all the space and prospect that the city swallowed up. I can well imagine how a child imprisoned and nearly suffocating in the clutter where two miserable, stunted little streets met, would suddenly conceive a frantic need for perspective that would dictate the entire course of his life.

IV.

THE PASSION FOR PERSPECTIVE

O ne night, Paolo Uccello had deserted the marital bed. His
wife, awakened by the empty place, made her way to his
studio and tenderly berated him for these oft-repeated defections.

"Oh, how wondrous fair is perspective!" was the painter's only
response.

***

A hundred and fifty years after these sleepless Italian nights, the passion for geometry had not subsided.[2] Hats off to the early seventeenth century! The desire for knowledge was spreading. Every
month, like mushrooms after the storm of civil conflicts, learned
societies were springing up. One of them, whose discussions focused
on the sciences, was presided over by Father Mersenne. A plow-
man's son, born in 1588, he studied at the Sorbonne and was then received into the monastery of the Order of Minims, just behind the
Place Royale (now called Place des Vosges). Without ever leaving
his place of retreat, he spent his time in correspondence. Every
blesséd day and night, he wrote, to all the learned men of Europe.
Questioning elicited answers, disputes engendered debates, and little
by little the new conception of our world was hammered out.

Descartes, a regular member of the Minims group, was twenty-six years old when he was visited by a flash of inspiration: mathematics is the language of the universe. To discover the laws governing nature we have but to follow where the logic of mathematics leads. This appeal to the generalized use of Reason, even for proving the existence of God, broke with the centuries-old practices of scholastic theology.

Another who came to the Minims was Pascal. Reason, in his opinion, does not have all the answers. When rational intelligence has taken us as far down the road as it can go, we are left with an unyielding central core of anguish and doubt. The best-ordered human construct will always retain some admixture of baroque irregularity, the gaiety that refuses to be consoled.

And, as is always the case, an era's metaphysics will be reflected in its gardens.

* * *

Jean Pèlerin, called le Viator (1435–1524), suffered from the same affliction as Uccello. Whenever he could snatch a few leisure moments from his multifarious duties as church canon, diplomat, and member of King Louis XI's Royal Council, he would lose himself in the mysteries of drawing. By 1505, he considered his knowledge sufficiently advanced to publish forty woodcuts, representing buildings, each accompanied by a commentary in two eight-syllable lines of verse: *De Artificiali Perspectiva,* an early treatise on perspective.

This pioneer work was followed by an endless stream of manuals, applied to every possible sphere of activity, joinery and cabinetmaking, marquetry and inlay work, stonecutting, gnomonics (the science of sundials) . . . Gardens were no exception. Jacques Androuet Du Cerceau's book *Les Plus Excellents Bâtiments de France* (1576) and Salomon de Caus's *La Perspective avec la raison des ombres et des miroirs* (1612) were to become universally accepted teaching authorities.

These thinkers, these works, were the context of Le Nôtre's professional training.

The curriculum taught under Father Bourdin at the Collège de Clermont (which later became Louis-le-Grand High School) is a good illustration of the prevailing outlook:

> The course in mathematics is composed of six main parts: arithmetic, geometry, music, enginry or mechanicke, optic and cosmography, which six have also their several parts . . . Geometry has these: the speculative, the practical, the deductive, the applicative, the projective, the military, etc.
>
> 1. The *speculative* considers the nature of geometric figures and bodies;
> 2. The *practical* constructs all manner of figures;
> 3. The *deductive* seeks to discover all the figures and *triangle* elements, reasoning from those few elements already known;
> 4. The *applicative* applies the *deductive* to deter-

mining *heights, distances, areas,* the breadth of a river or field;

5. The *projective* constructs figures and bodies *similar* to those presented to it, and in such *proportion* as may be desired;

6. The *military* is concerned with the *fortification* of strongholds, sieges.[3]

A remarkable age, indeed, when the teaching of mathematics, seen as combining authentic mental training and practical apprenticeship, included the study of music!

In that climate of opinion, perspective became much more than simply an object of learning. It turned into a kind of religion; it unleashed passions. People would happily have cut each other's throats over it, in the finest French tradition.

Girard Desargues[4] was an architect and lived in Lyons. He had no patience with the profusion of treatises that, instead of presenting an actual method for drawing, most often offered just a cookbook hodgepodge of recipes for particular problems. Desargues put forward a theorem applicable to every situation: "If two triangles have their vertices collinear with a point O, then the straight lines extending their sides intersect at three collinear points A, B, and C." All ye of nonmathematical bent, simply grasp what this implies: any spatial figure can be reduced to two dimensions. Perspective had found its keystone.

Poor Girard Desargues!

Scarcely had his essay appeared when it was plagiarized by the Reverend Father Du Breuil, a prominent Jesuit. The poor devil from Lyons stuck printed protests up on the walls of Paris, but to no avail. A tussle with the Company of Jesus was an unequal contest. Nor were Desargues's troubles at an end. A fellow by the name of Curabelle launched a vicious attack against him. Resorting once again to posted placards, our man responded with "The shameful behavior of Master Curabelle." His antagonist came back with "The pathetic weakness of Master Desargues . . ."

The controversy would continue until the opponents had died.

V

THE GREAT CONCOURSE

C atherine de Médicis had intended to link the Louvre to her newly built Tuileries Palace, five hundred fifty yards away. Her idea was that the connecting walkway, to be built along the shore of the Seine and called the Waterside Gallery, would allow her to escape whatever inclemencies the weather might bring. More especially, she would be able to flee discreetly whenever civil unrest set Paris ablaze once more. Her death in 1589 had temporarily brought construction to a halt. It was speedily resumed by Henri IV almost as soon as he had settled into his capital city, and he gave the project broader scope. On 1 January 1608, the longest gallery in Europe was formally inaugurated. It had four levels and ended in a new wing, called the Pavillon de Flore, built onto the Tuileries Palace.

Whereas the ground floor went to accommodate soldiers, Henri IV made the mezzanine and second floor available to the most renowned or promising artists and craftsmen in the kingdom. He offered each one a place to live and a workshop. Within weeks, every creator and inventor in France was arranging his paintbrushes or saws, his styluses or lathes, there in the Louvre. This permanent exhibition rapidly became a favorite promenade for the citizens of

Paris. When he came into the world, the Le Nôtre child did not just have a park on his doorstep to teach him about nature. Almost as close at hand, there was displayed for his benefit a living encyclopedia, a jumbled assembly of skills and knowledge, the excitement of a permanent workshop going day and night, and excellence in every possible guise. The sounds of sketching and planing, of gem setting and polishing, of screw turning, measuring, altering, sculpting, and portrait painting, mingled to produce an unlikely cacophony . . . And all the while a host of gawkers, among them the occasional buyer, made comments, asked questions, haggled over prices, and were mightily entertained.

Along with the traditional artists and craftsmen—painters, jewelers, skilled woodworkers, clockmakers, locksmiths—Henri IV and his successors brought to the Louvre a new breed of person, very representative of that era and its passion for knowledge: engineers. Leonardo da Vinci had shown the way with those inspired sketches of his (Archimedes' screw, the military tank, the revolving parabolic bridge, and the innumerable drafts for machines: machines for forging metal, for carding, weaving, woodcutting, rubble clearing . . .). His successors, handymen-scientists, came to the Louvre to display their latest inspirations in the way of "mathematical devices."[5] One of them was especially well respected among people who worked with terrain, whether landscape gardeners or military tacticians. His name was Philippe Danfrie, and he was the inventor of the graphometer. This instrument used chains laid in triangles and the laws of geometry to measure distance between the various reference points in a given space. A graphometer combined two distinct objects. The *viewer* was a horizontal circle fitted with eyepieces and mounted on a tripod. You set it firmly into the ground and you aimed it. The *protractor*, much like the one we remember from school days, was used for recording on paper the data thus observed, starting with the degree of each angle on which all calculations would be based.

Every year brought a fresh batch of new contrivances, which professionals in the various fields would not on any account have missed seeing.

So it was that the Louvre paved the way for Versailles. The guilds learned to work together, in an ambience of mutual respect. Lifelong friendships were born. And when Louis XIV came, like some new pharaoh, to set in motion his vast, encompassing projects, these armies of workers would be ready.

Not until Diderot and his *Encyclopédie* would there be another such convergence of theoretical and practical knowledge, which saw scientists, creative artists, and skilled craftsmen rub shoulders with no thought for professional superiority or pride of place. But the writings and drawings of Diderot and his crew can hardly be compared to the atmosphere of that Waterside Gallery, where human intelligence was on public display, where boundaries were abolished between the mental and the manual, where art, knowledge, and know-how walked hand in hand, where a dream of the whole man was made real.

* * *

Following hard upon their masters, apprentices invaded the palace. They knew the regulation Henri IV had decreed: five years of toil at the Louvre gave you the right to letters patent confirming you as master craftsman, entitled to practice your trade wherever you might choose.

At fifteen or sixteen years of age, André Le Nôtre entered this little world where everyone was at once relentlessly hardworking and utterly unruly. He was admitted to the studio of Simon Vouet.

Born in 1590, painter Simon Vouet was an extreme case of early-blooming talent. At fourteen, he was already traveling through western Europe and Turkey, doing portraits of persons of quality. He soon settled in Rome, the hotbed of budding artists, where wealthy patrons competed with noble families in hopes that Vouet might deign to accept their commissions, especially for works with religious subjects: crucifixions, visions of the Virgin . . . Word of his abilities reached the ears of Louis XIII, who recalled him to Paris and set him up in the Louvre.

Vouet's workshop quickly became the studio most sought after by aspiring young painters. Under his clear, generously bestowed guidance, they took part in the intense artistic activity of the master, as, one after another, most of the grand town houses then under construction in Paris were put into his hands for decorating. They also learned to draw tapestry cartoons, an art that Simon Vouet revived, bringing to it a great breath of fresh Baroque air and free composition.

In this studio, Le Nôtre struck up personal friendships, among others with a certain Charles Le Brun, an apprentice like himself. André Le Nôtre was to remain at the Louvre for six years, remarkable constancy in so young a man. Steadfastness of character, if you will, but also a passion for what he was doing. Painting or landscape gardening? The time had come to choose, and either choice would be a wrench. Gardening won; family tradition was not to be set aside in that day and age. And the laws of family tradition were as strong, its dynasties as well established, for gardeners as they were for noblemen.

VI

RHIZOMES AND EMBROIDERY

King Louis XIII's written decision is dated 26 January 1637:

In consideration of the good and commendatory report we have received respecting the person of our *dear and well-beloved* André Le Nôtre, and being fully persuaded of his sufficient *loyalty* and *probity, his experience in the matter of gardens,* and his faithful diligence and reliability, for these and other reasons we have given and granted and do hereby give and grant to the aforesaid, as attested by our signature subscribed in our hand, the position and office of gardener for our Tuileries gardens, which post is presently filled by his father Jean Le Nostre, the same having resigned this office in favor of his son, on condition, however, that the father retain right of reversion. And we further enjoin the sieur de Congis, captain of the aforesaid Tuileries, that when it shall have appeared to him that the aforenamed is of *good character, living decently* in the apostolic and

> *Roman Catholic faith* and when he shall have
> taken and received from him the oath customarily
> required in such cases, he shall in our name set
> and establish the said André Le Nostre the son in
> full and immediate possession of the aforemen-
> tioned office of gardener for our aforesaid
> Tuileries gardens.[6]

For a long time yet, the Tuileries would be dominated by families that grew and spread through the place like so many rootstocks,
so many rhizomes. Jean Le Nostre succeeded his father Pierre and
passed his office on to *his* son André. Jean's daughter Élisabeth married Pierre Desgots, another gardener: they would have a son,
Claude, who later inherited from André, André's own offspring having died in childhood. Jean's second daughter Françoise was to wed
Simon Bouchard, the man in charge of the Orangerie. When God
wrested Simon from the bosom of his loved ones, this same
Françoise, helped by her two sons, took over management of the
royal orange trees . . . Similarly with the Mollet family: they were to
be solidly entrenched through four generations. And Claude,
founder of the Mollet dynasty, would have a wife, and his wife
would have a godson . . . André Le Nôtre.

Rhizome: from the Greek *rhizoma,* "thing that is rooted; the un-
derground stem of hardy plants, producing adventitious roots and
leaved overground stems."

* *
 *

André's years of drawing and painting in the Louvre had not taken him far from his birthplace, in fact a bare two hundred *toises,* let us say four hundred and thirty yards. And now at twenty-four he was coming back so his father could hand over the keys to the garden. One Le Nôtre had been replaced by another. Nothing had changed. His "works and days" were as like as peas in a pod to the days, each with its labors, that he had known since childhood.

He took to wife Françoise, daughter of François Langlois, permanent member of the French Artillery Council. Fortifications and gardens, the poliorcetic and the botanic, the art of laying siege and the art of laying out gardens. When it's all in the family, professional practices are bound to be compared. Since the development of artillery, fortification had become in large measure an occupation based on landscape.

Vauban was born twenty years after Le Nôtre. But even before he came on the scene, there had been radical changes in the way strategists thought about fortified towns. Gone were the crenellated city walls, the high towers and keeps, all vulnerable to cannonballs. Military construction had long since been molded to the constraints of the terrain on which it stood and in which it was embedded. This was another matter that the Jesuits had pondered more deeply than anyone else, and a treatise by the Reverend Father Fournier sums up contemporary knowledge in the field.

A first child was born: Jean-François. A first child died. Two more would be given by the Lord and by the Lord immediately taken away again. If an inheritance was to be left, André could not count on having direct heirs to receive it. From morn till night, Le Nôtre gardened. That is to say, he drew plans and gave instructions. Not for him the wheelbarrows and dibbles. Le Nôtre embellished; he embroidered.

Parterres de broderies, embroidery-work flower beds, were not a recent creation. The Renaissance had delighted in them, before Le Nôtre. The seventeenth century, likewise, doted on those arabesques that brought together two of the century's passions, vegetation and ornamentation. There was actually an instructional garden, on the Île Notre-Dame, where people were taught to classify plants and identify them. Ladies and their embroiderers went there to get ideas for patterns.

And was it all terribly frustrating for this man who carried inside him the great open spaces that would one day make him famous? There is no evidence that he was champing at the bit, except perhaps that he admitted late in life to some slight feeling of contempt for these boring professional exercises. Le Nôtre, according to Saint-Simon, disdained parterres, those sections in a garden "where nobody ever walks [and which] were of no use to anyone but nursemaids unable to leave their young charges unattended, hence obliged to roam the flower beds only with their eyes, admiring them from upper-story windows." We can sympathize with his surfeit of interlacing loops: André Le Nôtre had spent twenty years of his life knitting, using boxwood shrubs for yarn.

VII

"SOMEDAY MY PRINCE WILL COME"

I f no one commissions a gardener's work, it stays in his portfolio. To become a reality, the dream needs space and it needs money. More than any of the other arts, landscape gardening is dependent on goodwill backed by large and lasting pecuniary resources.

Le Nôtre climbed the rungs of the hierarchy one by one, to become in 1648 Designer of the King's Plantations and Gardens and in 1656 Superintendent of Buildings. He broadened his botanical lore, continued to hobnob with engineers at the Louvre Gallery, and met the great contemporary architects including the greatest of all, François Mansart. And he waited. He waited in the best possible way: with no impatience, no gnawing desire, not even knowing he was waiting, absorbed as he was in each day's work. But deep inside him was hope; the hope that a powerful personage driven by ambition would give him a chance to show what he could do.

As his reputation grew, a few private individuals began offering him their estates to redesign and develop. These did not as yet represent projects of particularly great scope, just opportunities to get experience and supplement his regular income (for the royal emoluments could hardly be described as generous). Gaston d'Orléans, for instance, sought Le Nôtre's help with the grounds of his Luxembourg Park. It amounted to designing variations on themes already conceived by other people. Just like at the Tuileries. A nice token of esteem, but frustrating having to follow meekly where someone else had led.

What finally opened the gates of destiny for him was friendship.

Despite his long sojourn in Rome, Charles Le Brun had never forgotten Le Nôtre. Their shared memories of the Grand Gallery at the Louvre, being schooled by Simon Vouet, were a permanent bond. Now an opportunity arose that would mean working together once again. Only this time they were being asked, not to sit side by side copying the old masters as in those days long ago, but to create a masterpiece of their own, from scratch.

I've found the powerful patron you've been looking for, said Le Brun. He's bought a hundred-and-ninety-acre tract of land. Le Vau is doing the mansion. I've taken on the paintings and sculptures. The gardens, the gardens-to-be, are there waiting for you: digging has just begun.

* * *

The person who had set out to dazzle the kingdom and its king was a nobleman, the most outgoing and socially brilliant of them all. And his very name, Fouquet, "squirrel" in the dialect of the west of France, suggested that here was someone with reserves at his disposal. The office entrusted to him by Mazarin in 1653—superintendent of finance—reinforced his surname.

Fouquet was a born tightrope walker. Better than anyone else, he could dance nimbly above the yawning void. Nothing gave him greater pleasure than to thumb his nose at bankruptcy. He juggled from dawn to dusk, on his own behalf or that of the State. A hundred times he used incredible strategems to ward off collapse of a royal treasury bled dry by war and civil disorder. As to his personal fortune, it was as vast as his debts. Never mind that his situation was shaky! With his genius for unlimited borrowing, every wild extravagance was perfectly permissible.

Fouquet distrusted Mazarin, whose favor was fickle. Hoping that one day he might negotiate with his benefactor on equal terms, Fouquet was forever buying up lands in Brittany. Soon, from Saint-Brieuc to Rosporden, from Dol to Concarneau, a goodly part of the region belonged to him. So did the marquessate of Belle-Île, which he contrived to acquire. He secretly turned the island into a fortress, the pivotal component of the "Breton redoubt" that would later be grounds for accusing Fouquet of rebellion and lèse-majesté.

Safe from attack on the west, he could devote his full attention to regaling society and making a display. "Insatiable where the fair sex was concerned," as Father de Choisy put it, Fouquet could also appreciate other pleasures. He assembled around him a peerless circle of scholars and cultured men of letters: Scarron, Scudéry, Corneille, Molière, Perrault, La Fontaine, Quinault, all regular visitors to his estate at Saint-Mandé.

Twenty-five years earlier, Mme. de Rambouillet had set an example for enjoyment of these refined leisure pursuits. You came to her town house seeking conversation; you came in order to learn, and laugh, and to cultivate friendship as an art, indeed the supreme art. Especially, you came for a taste of freedom, to escape the "wretched discipline" that Richelieu was imposing on the Louvre and on France. Voiture, a poet cruelly and unjustly neglected by posterity, was "the heart and soul of this circle." He was a genius in the art of living, but scant trace remains of his existence, other than in Tallement des Réaux's *Historiettes,* or in books by Marc Fumaroli, our inimitable wayfarer through treasures of the past that put the present era to shame. Fouquet, with his generosity, charm, and thoughtfulness, had succeeded in forming a similar "circle."

Having his own intellectual and artistic coterie was not enough. He meant to dazzle the polite world with a physical place.

And so was born the idea of Vaux-le-Vicomte, whose splendor would be Fouquet's downfall . . . and Le Nôtre's stroke of luck.

* * *

Success that comes late can be like the overture to certain operas. From the opening bars, it's all there. The artist has waited so long for his big chance that when it comes he is fully prepared. He has cherished so many vain hopes that he realizes how rare and fleeting is this moment. When at last he is granted an opportunity to show what he can do, he gives his all.

So it was with André Le Nôtre at Vaux. By the time Fouquet put his demesne in Le Nôtre's hands, the gardener was forty years old. Into this enterprise he would pour his soul. He would produce a work that was at once the epitome of his craft and a masterpiece, the ultimate expression of the French-style garden. But far removed from the caricature conjured up in people's minds by that phrase. A French garden is assumed to be boring, obvious, fully revealed at first sight, when in fact it likes nothing better than saving up to surprise you. It is supposed to be a set piece, petrified, unchanging ever, whereas in fact its reflecting water surfaces are the favorite haunts of the ephemeral. It is thought to be rigid, frigid, inhuman, but in fact perspective properly handled is the most comforting of landscapes. Everyone believes such a garden will be hostile to nature, though in fact what it does is arrange for nature to converse with the mind.

Setting out on our walk, let's allow ourselves to be guided by appearances: they will fool us every time.[7] Facing away from the château, we head toward the line of grottoes with statues of human figures, away at the far end of the vista. Do your eyes tell you the central pathway is straight? That's your  first mistake: the path widens gradually to offset foreshortening with its tendency to shrink the horizon. Do you think you are walking along a flat surface? Those are your second and third mistakes:

twice you will come out onto terraces overlooking but masking ornamental pools one level down. Well, at least the grottoes are still standing peacefully at eye level, waiting for you to reach them. Another double mistake. One more step and you would have fallen into the green waters of a very long canal that was quite invisible a moment earlier. And as for your grottoes, they gaze appealingly up at you from the bottom of a hollow. They can scarcely be called formal, there amid the rustling of leaves, but they do put you in mind of the corollary to theorem number ten in Euclidean geometry: "When a surface is situated below eye level, its more distant parts will appear to be higher."

Somewhat annoyed at having been deceived so many times, you make your way around the canal, taking comfort in one certainty at least: the sculptures. Tangible and undeniable, nobody can say they don't exist. The crowning jest. All that you find, by way of solemn, antique marble statuary, is seven stalagmites, seven vulgar limestone concretions. True, a pair of imposing personages are eyeing you disdainfully, one from either side. If you haven't recognized them, you're missing the ultimate ironic touch. One of them represents father Nile, king of rivers; the other deifies the Anqueil, a tiny stream converted to a canal by thousands of workmen with shovels.

The walk began not half an hour ago, and already you're completely confused about what is real and what isn't.

As for the château, you can turn around to find it perfectly reflected on the water, but come the lightest breeze and it has disappeared, swallowed up with no survivors. Rotundas, domes, windows tall and windows oval, all have vanished without a trace.

A kind of giddiness comes over you, as at a masked or costumed ball; you feel lighter, less scrunched up in yourself. It wouldn't take much for you to wave yourself good-bye and go off to hook up with someone else, God knows who. Besides, the "confessional" awaits your pleasure: three stone-lined arches, well suited to amorous adventures. All around you is the forest, with nothing separating it from the park. Pathways make beckoning channels of light through the trees; you have but to heed the call. Classicism is not as properly behaved as people think.

Lovemaking is like that: you move along, guided by appearances beneath appearances, until you arrive at the naked flesh and find that its texture is not what you expected. Woe to the garden, and woe to the woman, who holds no surprises in reserve for the visitor.

And then peace returns. You have reached the grassy amphitheater overhanging the canal. In the distance, close to the skyline, the Farnese Hercules is watching over you, while a fountain—the Gerbe—plays in the sunlight. You've had your fill of surprises and now's the time for a rest. You savor the interplay of lines and the visual echo of the slopes as they call and answer one another from end to end of the park. Voices as of a choir reach you, in a harmony of shapes, mute music, of a kind that only the eye can perceive.

> Places so beauteous, I would have thought
> That only enchantment these spells could have wrought
> Had not Vaux shown me such things can be.
>
> —La Fontaine

* *
*

Five years of unceasing labor, twelve miles of piping and six of tree-covered walks, as many as ten thousand men laboring on the site at one time . . . Saws, paintbrushes, and spades were still hard at work when, in the late afternoon of 17 August 1661, the carriage bearing Louis XIV passed through the gates. Fouquet was there waiting for him, as was the entire royal court. Thereupon began the most sophisticated festivities of the century, festivities lasting eight hours. Vying in excellence were the arts at the pinnacle of perfection: theater, music, ballet, painting, cabinetmaking and marble work, gardens and fountains, cuisine and fireworks, sculptures and gowns . . .

> The music, the waters, the lusters, and stars
> All strove at Vaux, which might give fullest measure
> For the king's pleasure . . .

But the king in question, as wonder succeeded wonder for his delectation, was more and more consumed with envy. He was personally humiliated by all this luxury, crushed by all this elegance, tormented by these canals, fountains and cascades: Versailles had no water.

La Fontaine described it all to his friend Maucroix, then sojourning in Rome. The poet alternated between verse and prose, so my reader will realize how out of place a paraphrase would be.

> There was a magnificent supper, a first-rate play, a
> most entertaining ballet, and fireworks very differ-
> ent from the ones that marked the Royal Arrival.

All things that might our senses please
Those proffered entertainments seemed.
Of place and master worthy these
And also of their Majesties
If aught could so be deemed.

At two o'clock in the morning, as Louis XIV, beside himself with anger, was issuing orders for his return to Versailles, a terrible storm broke and two horses were killed.

I did not imagine that this account was to have so piteous and tragical an ending.

Twenty days later, La Fontaine took pen in hand to write Maucroix again:

My dear friend, I cannot comment on what you have written me touching my business affairs; these are of less moment to me than the misfortune that has just befallen the Superintendent. He is under arrest, and the king speaks against him in the most vituperative fashion, to the point of claiming he has in his possession written evidence that will hang him.

In Nantes, on 5 September, d'Artagnan, lieutenant of the Grays, the first company of musketeers, acting on written instruction from Louis XIV, had arrested Fouquet.

•

* * *

Fouquet was no sooner imprisoned than Louis XIV looted his estates. Furniture, paintings, books, tapestries, even the statues took to the road, destination all too well known, in covered wagons, under armed escort. The seizure extended to people as well as possessions. The whole team was snatched away and by autumn they were in Versailles. Le Vau the architect; Villedo and Bergeron the master builders; Le Brun the painter; Girardon, Augier, and Lourant the cabinetmakers, La Quintinie the horticulturist . . . Included in this rape was Le Nôtre. A dazzled, willing Le Nôtre. What, after all, was a money-juggling superintendent compared to the king of France?

* * *

Did Le Nôtre ever come back to Vaux? The place smacked of treason, the splenetic monarch had spies everywhere, and our gardener knew when prudence was called for . . . And yet I can picture him going back, toward the end of his life.

An old man, walking toward that spot where suddenly there is a canal. He moves at a leisurely pace through this perfect landscape of his own creating. He knows better than anyone else that all his later works are a commentary on this one. In Versailles, he worked on a grander scale. In Chantilly, he gave fuller treatment to water. At Saint-Cloud, he was more imaginative in exploiting the site and its

complexities . . . But the heart and basic rule book for all these vari-
ants were already present at Vaux.

And before he set off, back to Versailles and the company of his
friend the Sun King, did it perhaps occur to our visitor that he
should secretly give thanks to the squirrel?

Versailles goes back a long way before Versailles. To find the roots of the dream requires a careful scrutiny of the late 1640s, when a host of angry currents began to rock the kingdom. The Great Nobles were reacting angrily to royal power and the decline in their revenues. Incumbents of high office reacted angrily to the emergence of an institutionalized state that was progressively eating away their privileges. The *parlementaires,* dispensers of royal justice, reacted angrily to the measures being decreed by Mazarin and dreamed of exercising control over the government. As for the populace, its poor wretched masses reacted angrily to the skyrocketing pressures of taxation (a fourfold increase in fifteen years). Grievance was piled on grievance, until the Fronde uprisings broke out. There was revolt, then riot, and Paris awoke one morning to streets bristling with barricades. A threatening crowd surged forward toward the Palais-Cardinal (the present Palais-Royal). No ditch or moat protected it. An irreparable potential act of regicide was narrowly avoided. Louis XIV had just turned ten. He conceived that day a fear of his capital city, along with deep loathing for all these civil disorders. Neither of these feelings would ever abate.

And the troubles went on. It is three in the morning of 6 January 1649. Maréchal de Villeroy awakens Louis, dresses him in the dark, and carries the child away in his arms. They leave the Palais-Royal by a secret door and climb into a carriage where Queen Mother Anne of Austria is waiting. She has decided to try and reach Saint-Germain; there they will have the protection of the prince de Condé, who has remained loyal. At first light of day, mother and son settle into the gloomy empty castle. As it is no longer in use, all the furniture has been removed. No wood for the fireplace, no sheets for the beds, no panes in half the windows, this at a time of year when chunks of ice are floating down the Seine.

The great goals of life, compensations more often than not, are forged in childhood. It is a safe bet that the dream of Versailles was born in Saint-Germain, during that winter when France was frozen to her very marrow. Some day I will build a castle for the sun, some day the Great Nobles, all the proud, arrogant nobles from across the kingdom, will come crowding to my castle to bow before me, sweeping their hats across the floor in my royal presence.

✳ ✳ ✳

A long decade had passed and the scene had changed. The prime minister was dead, the superintendent locked up. A young man of twenty-five wanted to show that he was king. Terrorized by what had happened at Vaux, the Great Nobles had got the message. Europe was learning to fear him. A royal carousel would shortly convince the people. "Carousel," *carrus solis:* chariot of the sun.[8]

The event was staged in the gardens of La Grande Mademoiselle, duchesse de Montpensier, between the Louvre and the Tuileries Palace. For the tournament itself, there were viewing stands packed with five thousand privileged spectators, but Parisians turned out en masse along the parade route. ("No one has stayed home," it was said that day, 5 June 1662.) Well might they stare at the procession of 655 horsemen, plumed and feathered, organized into five brigades. The king led the first of these, the Brigade of Romans. His imperial robe was embroidered in gold and spangled with diamonds. His silver helmet bore a crest of fiery plumes from which four herons protruded. The escutcheon represented a sun inscribed with the device *Ut vidi vici,* "I no sooner saw than I conquered."

The other brigades were no less extravagant. Monsieur, the king's oldest brother, led a company of Persians wearing crimson bonnets and white plumes. The prince de Condé was followed by blue, black, and silver Turks. His son, the duc d'Enghien, was emperor to the men of India, a brown-hued crew richly decked out in yellow and black. The duc de Guise and his "savages from the American wilds" brought up the rear. The duke himself was costumed as a fish, silver scales covering his body, fins at the end of his sleeves, coral bonnet. A tiger skin interwoven with green velvet caparisoned his horse. His squire had been swallowed up by a long-maned dragon, while his page had changed into a monkey. Completing the assemblage was a troop of satyrs with unicorns for steeds . . .

The people of Paris greeted this equestrian opera with acclaim; they swooned with admiration. Everyone truly loved the monarch who could command such magnificent spectacles; he must surely be master of all the world.

For a full three days, the five teams would meet in contest: tourneys, carousels, tilting at the ring; an unforgettable pageant of farewell to feudalism. And a political masterstroke built on an understanding of human nature. By playing on their vanity, Louis had forced the Great Nobles to make public show of their own submission. To the cheers of the multitude, the duc d'Enghien repeatedly brandished his shield. Painted upon it were a planet and the four words *Magno de lumine lumen,* "Light from a greater light." The motto of allegiance.

* * *

Hitherto the nobles of highest rank had had eyes only for themselves. Now Louis XIV was to present them with a spectacle such that they would not consider turning their gaze away from their king even for a moment. The Great Nobles, in the shadow and remoteness of their several provinces, amassed monies and hatched schemes. Some of them he would ruin; on others he would heap favors. The fortunes of each and every one were to depend henceforth solely on his royal pleasure.

Above all, he placed them in forced residence—*his* residence—so he would never lose sight of them. They gazed upon him; he looked upon them: the eye became the chief weapon of politics. From morn till eve, a courtier must strive first and foremost to be seen. "A glance or a word from the King, who was not lavish with either, was a precious token that attracted attention and envy," wrote Saint-Simon, who bemoaned his own fate: "Only by chance did his eyes ever turn in my direction."

The *Mémoires* of Primi Visconti, quoted by José Cabanis,[9] explain precisely how Louis XIV's system operated: "When the King condescends to glance at someone, that person considers himself a made man and brags about it, saying to others: 'The King looked at me.' You may be sure that the King is no fool! How many are those he pays in no other coin than by looking their way!"

Le Nôtre could only rejoice at this primacy of the eye. After all, are not gardens the kingdom of that which is seen?

* * *

The Ministry of Culture was born on 3 February 1663. On that date,[10] Colbert brought together, at his home, four individuals on whom he could count. There was Charles Perrault, who for the moment was indolently employed by his brother Pierre, Receiver-General of Finances for Paris; in his ample leisure moments, he produced for special occasions versified pieces, which the king had appreciated. Then Jean de la Chapelle, an old literary critic. Next, theologian Amable de Bourzéis. Lastly, the abbé Cassagne, preacher. The first assignment entrusted to them by Colbert was of the utmost importance: they would choose the mottoes and emblems to be engraved on all medals and royal buildings. That is how this "petite Académie" came later on to be called the Académie des inscriptions et belles-lettres.

The group of four was very soon given another, more general responsibility: propaganda. Art and artists were to be enlisted in the king's service.

The Little Academy met at Colbert's residence twice weekly, on Tuesdays and Fridays. Between meetings, under Perrault's direction, the quartet exacted, examined, expurgated, and rewarded.

The Little Academy ruled over the big ones, placing its hirelings among the membership of those bodies: Lully in the Académie royale de danse, Le Brun in the Académie de peinture et de sculpture, the Reverend Father Du Hamel in the Académie de sciences (1666). For the Académie française, founded in 1634, "their" man was Perrault himself. And it was Perrault again who kept *the list:* some sixty or eighty lucky recipients of royal largesse. There was no other way for artists to make their living in an era when author's rights did not exist.

* * *

Whereas writing, painting, sculpture, music, and the royal medallions[II] made separate contributions to the task of eulogizing, gardens could present an allegorical system embracing them all. And it could situate that system in a defined space where anyone might walk. And set it into the weather cycle: as season followed season, the legend went on uninterrupted.

"I want you for Versailles."

The rapture of a mere mortal who has been put in charge of such an undertaking defies imagination. Actually to receive this commission from the king, not merely from an all-powerful human being, but—remembering that the seventeenth century did not distinguish between secular and sacred authority—from a divinity incarnate! And the garden he was being called on to create was the garden of the monarchy itself. In planning it, he would be telling the new story of the kingdom and its link with heaven. A prospect dizzying enough to stagger any man.

* * *

On a day in 1983, I saw Ieoh Ming Pei coming out of François Mitterrand's office. The president of the Republic had just put in his hands the Louvre, with instructions to make it into "the world's most beautiful museum" (French politicians have never been known for modesty). All my life I shall remember the Chinese-born architect's round glasses and childlike smile. We walked back to the gates together. Or rather I walked; he was floating. Never had visitor trod the graveled courtyard with a lighter step.

So I can picture Le Nôtre after his interview with the king. The man wending his way home that evening through the streets did not take the shortest route. He strayed a little. It was the only way to regain his composure. He followed the banks of the Seine where porters, longshoremen, *faisaient grève,* not in today's sense of being on strike but idling on the banks, waiting for work, for a ship that wanted loading or unloading. Turning west, he wandered aimlessly in the wooded area where as a child he had encountered his first rabbits and wild boars. He said hello to the birds in the aviary, paid a final visit to the flower beds, whose every bulb had been planted under his supervision. Nostalgia and pride struggled for primacy in his heart. He asked his beloved Tuileries Gardens to forgive the long infidelity that was going to keep him busy in another place.

IX.

A BOOK TWENTY-FIVE HUNDRED
ACRES BIG

Artists and men of learning had been called together for the purpose of mythmaking. And so they stirred up a brew; they stirred it over a slow heat as though in a giant stew-pot; into the mix they stirred present time and ancient past, history and legend, Homer, Ovid, and the moderns, the religions of yesteryear and revealed Truth . . .

Out of this mad, meticulous cookery would be born the Sun King. Louis XIV is the son of God, he is the anointed of the Lord, he is the Christ, but no more than that. Even the great Bossuet draws the line there. He says to the kings of the earth: "You are gods," but he cannot say to them: "You are God."[12] Since the role of God is (unfortunately) off-limits, why not be chief among the gods, that is to say Apollo, son of Zeus and Latona, habitual lover, tireless seducer of nymphs, lord of music and the dance, expert in the art of prophecy, intrepid hunter of dragons, satyrs and cyclopes, master of universal harmony?

The monarch's chamber, in the exact middle of the château, was also the heart of the park (and the center of the world), the magical spot where the north-south, or water axis, and the east-west, or Sun axis, met and crossed. Thanks to Louis-Apollo the two opposing elements were reconciled.

The story told in water started at the ornamental pond of les Suisses, to end at the Basin of Neptune, protector of Latona. Between these two points, subjects connected with Apollo unfolded like chapters: the role of the Tritons and Sirens, supporting the crown; the graceful Diana, sister of Apollo; monstrously ugly Python the serpent, slain by Apollo . . .

Perpendicular to the front and center of the castle, along a line made by the Allée Royale and the Grand Canal, would be the Sun cycle, with innumerable fables and allegories: Latona punishing rustics who had come to attack her by changing them into frogs, Apollo in person driving his chariot with its four eagerly quivering

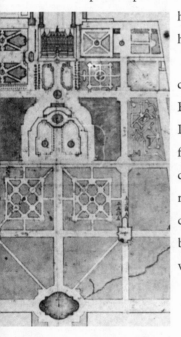

horses—the god of light launching forth upon his daily career across the heavens.

The groves of trees, too, the *bosquets,* were to convey messages for the Great Nobles to ponder. For example, the Bosquet de l'Encelade (1676). Poor Enceladus, quite unknown to us, but a figure familiar to those living in the seventeenth century: he was one of the giants who dared to rebel against Zeus. As a sculpture, he is shown crushed, despite his immense size, by a heap of boulders. *Frondeurs,* rebels of every ilk, look where I am looking: is the message clear?

Over the population of statues reigned the painter Le Brun. Working closely with the king and Colbert, Le Brun decided what themes would be depicted, and then commissioned the pieces, always choosing sculptors who were members of the Academy and so could be counted on to hew to the double line, aesthetic and political. Girardon, Le Hongre, Desjardins, Coysevox . . . their mission was strictly defined: promote the deification of Louis by peopling his garden with mythological heroes. Inanimate though they were, Antinous, Mercury, Venus, Bacchus, and Pluto would contribute to the glorification. Statues of emperors would be added, spiritual forebears of the French monarch in the order of their omnipotence: Alexander, Augustus, Septimus Severus.

Homage was also paid to Nature, but only to show how she was kept on a tight rein: hunting scenes, portraits of streams and rivers large or small, from the Loire to the Loiret and not forgetting the Saône.

Lastly, to make the moral complete, passions, virtues, and vices were brought to life in marble: fidelity (by Lefèvre), knavery (by Le Conte) . . .[13]

* * *

Versailles is a park, but it is equally *a book*. It is the bible through whose pages the god-king, resorting to every possible mode of narrative (allegories, digressions, secrets, surprises . . .) and flinging into the grand mix every sort of personage, whether divine, human or animal, tells who he is and fathers his own being.

**
    *

There are days when Versailles, however deep our devotion, is simply boring. We can't handle all that volume, all that empty space between the trees, all that silence, the broad sweep of all those avenues. It's too much. We are bored because we are uncultivated. As a result of our ignorance, we walk through a truncated work of art. Imagine being at an opera with the performers singing at the top of their lungs and not one aria reaching our ears. Pity those poor fountains and statues when we can no longer appreciate the stories they tell! Yet in their day they would certainly have made us see the merits of absolutism. For the fact is that Le Nôtre and his huge team brought off a prodigious feat: the successful fusion of extremely subtle art and totally unblushing propaganda. I defy you to name one other garden as political as this one. Only the eighteenth-century Manchu emperor Qian Long ever embarked on a comparable enterprise. At his two summer palaces of Yiheyuan and Yuan Ming-yuan, he set out to inscribe temporal power at the center of a cosmogony. Not, in the case of China, a Sun King, but a son of heaven, dwelling in the palace of benevolence and longevity . . . More than a hundred thousand seamen-workers, so it is said, labored to enlarge Lake Kunming. Which helps us understand how it happens that, of all the garden-parks in the world, only Versailles escapes contempt in Chinese eyes.

* * *

Over a period of twenty years, Louis XIV used Versailles as a structure to support his persona. On this framework he built a legend, slid neatly into it, and there charmed, enchanted, and captivated his world. The endless succession of fêtes at Versailles was directed to that end. One in particular, even more lavish than Fouquet's at Vaux, more complete in its symbolism than the Paris carousel of 1662, was an immoderate display of luxury and opulence, but at the same time a consummate exercise in political instruction. "The Pleasures of the Enchanted Isle" began on 7 May 1664. For an entire week, the six hundred privileged individuals admitted to Versailles would marvel at those "pleasures." Pleasures aimed at all the senses and raised to a pitch never reached before (the trial of Fouquet was drawing to a close; it was time to relegate the high-living superintendent to the depths of permanent oblivion). Musical pleasures, pleasures of the dance, of equestrian art and gastronomy, pleasures afforded by fireworks and the play of fountains, by theater and masquerade. The pleasures of watching as a spectator, or taking active part in every sort of sporting event. But none of these pleasures was innocent or gratuitous; each of them brought with it a message. And together they added up to an ideology.

The general narrative line, based on an episode from Ariosto's *Orlando Furioso,* was of course a mere pretext. Everyone must pay further homage, now and always, to the king, sole source of light (his costume sparkled with precious stones). All must hail the advent of the Golden Age, in its triumph over the century of iron. It must be made clear that henceforth the monarchy was picking up where feudal rights had left off. It was essential that modern France and its new wealth be on display (Colbert made sure of that). Implicit in every concert, every ballet, every formal procession, was an explanation or a warning. Day after day, on the Enchanted Isle, the royal discourse was clarified and crystalized. And so the fête went on until 12 May, when the black raiment of Tartuffe appeared in this brightly glistening atmosphere. The courtiers were struck as by a thunderbolt. The king was serving notice: he loathed hypocrisy, especially hypocrisy garbed as religion.

After the pleasures had drawn to a close, we can picture all the master craftsmen involved, Le Nôtre among them, clustered in happy exhaustion around Louis XIV. And a smiling Majesty proffering the words: "This time, they know who I am!" The politics of the eye was now established, and its setting was Versailles. It would continue, as fête followed fête, until the late 1670s.

X.

F R I E N D S H I P

What is it that produces a Golden Age, a sort of wave, suddenly lifting the arts of one particular country to heights of excellence?

It takes wealth, certainly. But so many opulent eras hoard and build without anything immortal to show for it. It takes mighty patrons, who have dreams and commission works. But what can their wild desires accomplish if there is no one, or hardly anyone, to answer the call? What explains the general mobilization, welling up from the very depths of one nation to transform a century—or part of a century—into a collective masterpiece? The genius of a few individuals is not enough; it has to be backed up by a vast pool of talents and knowledge whose repositories are men and women born roughly at the same time. Nor can they be unaware of each other's existence; they have to see one another, speak together, feel esteem— or the reverse—for each other, plan to work together, or compete with one another. In short, a Golden Age is the joint progeny of an entire generation.

However great our respect for the ties that bound Montaigne and La Boétie, literary friendships are not exclusive to the sixteenth

century. The century that followed was marked by outstanding examples as well. Racine (born in 1639) and La Fontaine (born in 1621)
met in Paris almost every day. They were soon joined by Molière
(1622) and Boileau (1636); the latter hastened to rent a room, on the
rue du Vieux-Colombier, where they could all meet. Another member of the group was Chapelle, a charming fellow, as fine a wit as he
was a keen connoisseur of brothels. They formed a quintet of inseparables: tragedian, fabulist, comedian, poet, and jolly dilettante. We
can surmise that occasionally their conversation shifted away from
the double topic of wine and women, and then they talked shop.
But, fruitful though such exchanges may be, literature is a solitary
pursuit.

Contrariwise, it requires a whole crowd of people to bring a castle
and its park out of a geographic wasteland.

* *
*

With his whole life given over to work, the only people Le Nôtre
could have as friends were those who shared his passion. To his passion he was dedicated, to his friends, devoted. And his existence was
built on unswerving faithfulness to two people at least: Claude
Desgots, his sister Élisabeth's son, who went with him everywhere,
including Rome, and Queen's Council member Jean-Baptiste de La
Quintinie, that jurist who, at about age thirty, became converted to
botany. Le Nôtre met him at Vaux and took him along to Versailles.

There he would entrust La Quintinie with a mission of peculiar delicacy: to satisfy a king who was extremely fond of fruit and especially pears, by creating the royal kitchen garden. It meant that a stinking marsh must somehow be turned into a marvel of elegance operating in defiance of the slowly changing seasons. Thanks to this plantation, in addition to pears—mouth-melting louise-bonne pears d'avranches, sugar-sweet doyennés-du-comice pears, and the like— an impatient monarch would be able to enjoy strawberries in January and figs in April.

But Le Nôtre had another accomplice who was even more important.

* * *

Since the days of the Waterside Gallery and Simon Vouet's studio, Le Nôtre and Le Brun had rarely been apart. True, the painter had gone off to train his eye in Rome, under the guidance of Poussin. But as soon as he was back they were seeing each other again. And no sooner was Le Brun hired by Fouquet than he sent for Le Nôtre. Side by side, they would fashion Vaux before moving on to Versailles. Three years for the superintendent, followed by thirty for the king. They were an ideally complementary twosome, one presiding over interiors, the other reigning over the out-of-doors. And together they oversaw the statuary, Le Brun placing the orders, Le Nôtre ordering the placement.

62   *   ANDRÉ LE NÔTRE

Both were tireless workers, and both had kept intact, from that memorable gallery of their younger days, a great enthusiasm for exchanges among the various craft guilds. Concurrently with his work as an artist and the innumerable projects that he managed, Le Brun was the guiding spirit of the Gobelins manufactory-cum-school. On the banks of the little Bièvre River, he received and trained an army of creative talents whose furniture and tapestries would decorate French palaces and fascinate Europe.

Both men were immensely skillful in their behavior at court. Le Brun was unbeatable for trading on his position in the Academy. He was its chancellor, its rector, and invented a post called "vice-protector," which he offered to his unflagging supporter Colbert. Le Brun had turned the king into a spectator: nothing gave His Majesty greater pleasure than to watch his chief painter at work . . . until it was time to go for a walk in the garden.

Both friends were deeply interested in the science of their day. Le Brun had read Descartes and his considerations on the brain, abode of the soul. He entered into philosophical debates, compared human and animal facial characteristics, explored the physical manifestations of feelings, and delivered, at the Louvre, a much-discussed lecture on physiognomy . . .

* * *

There is an enigma inherent in our Grand Siècle: how could the iron discipline imposed on the arts by Louis XIV and Colbert via their hirelings in the Little Academy, together with the steady, meticulously programmed mythologizing, produce so many masterpieces? Ordinarily, constraint and even more so political propaganda make poor bedfellows for artistic creation.

Perhaps the key to the Golden Age is to be found in friendship. These artists had bonds of affection going back to their youth, feelings that were a refuge for them, the answer to an insistent need.

XI.

A CANAL

Facing the château and extending westward were marshes crossed by a tiny stream called the Galie. You could contract fever if you lingered nearby and on certain days the stench made you want to throw up. One solution seemed imperative: drain the area and plant it to grass. Immediately upon his arrival at the site, Le Nôtre put forward a different idea.

Construction began in 1667. Four years later, a large cross-shaped canal occupied fifty-seven acres of terrain.

Fifty-seven acres in the middle of the park, providing all sorts of aquatic amusements. Gondolas, a gift from Venice, sailed upon the canal, as did a felucca from Naples, galleys, giant models (thirty-two guns) of ships of the line . . . a whole flotilla kept permanently ready for festivities, and manned by sixty tars prepared to weigh anchor at a moment's notice.

Today, the water no longer gives any hint of that bygone century. A few small, rented boats go round in circles, just like anywhere else, whether on the shores of the Marne or in the Bois de

Boulogne. The only swiftly gliding craft are the long boats from the Rowing Club, eights, fours, a double-scull. The oarsmen sit so low you would think they were on the water surface. On some autumn days, they vanish into the mist. For a few seconds the ear takes over from the eye; you can hear the rhythmic sound of the oarblades, the shouted encouragement of the coxswain. Then silence. Could it be that after 1,750 yards of canal they've picked up enough speed to go back in time? An optimistic hypothesis, but it helps me to a better understanding of their desperate exertions.

Also involved were fifty-seven acres of Île-de-France sky, for the canal was first and foremost a mirror. It captured the sun to please the king. But in our climes the sun doesn't always choose to appear. On those occasions, for want of a more noble object, the canal reflected clouds, light, whatever passed overhead, quickly or not so quickly depending on the wind, things purely ephemeral. Thanks to that canal in the park, the heavens and their whims became—meaning no disrespect to King Louis—the main characters in the story. And I like to tell myself that at any rate one thing about Versailles hasn't changed in three centuries, namely, change itself—thank the heavens.

XII

To Satisfy the Fountains

The seventeenth century was madly in love with water and saw the upward surge of fountains or the seething foam of cascades as a reflection of life and its turmoils. In images reflected on the surface of ponds or canals, and then suddenly blurred by the wind, people of the day liked to see a reminder of life's inherent fragility. Enamored as they were of line and perspective, nothing entertained them better than these optical fantasies. Religious as they were to their very core, they believed that all bodies of water, fresh or salt, communicated among themselves and that all were in communication with God. Prominent among those who shared this fascination was Descartes, as his essay *Les Météores* will testify. Lakes are the eyes of the ocean, perhaps even a part of God's gaze upon us. Water allowed the Grand Siècle to contemplate itself in its entirety and in all its facets, geometric and Baroque, passionately devoted to order and method but equally to surprise and illusion, mystical but addicted to pleasures and to gambling.

* * *

For Versailles, Louis XIV demanded water, more water, and still more water. Not in order to slake the thirst of plant life that was already being fed more than it could drink, but "to satisfy the fountains." This desire turned into an obsession. To please a woman could never cost as much; the natural ponds round about were poor, pathetic things, and no river crossed the site.

So began a venture that was to last half a century and allow engineers to play the role they like best: that of God fashioning the planet. Two hundred years later, in 1907, L. A. Barbet, a colleague of theirs in Public Works, would recount this epic of hydrology in minutest detail, after painstaking research. His fascinating book, unfortunately out of print, reduces the labors of Hercules to the job of a common weekend mister-fixit.[14]

First a pump was invented, more powerful than any yet seen. It lifted the water from Clagny, the only pond in the vicinity, up into a high tower dominating the garden. The rate of flow was hopelessly inadequate. So mills were built, reservoirs were constructed, the course of the Bièvre was altered. Alas, the fountains still cried out in want, and the king was becoming impatient. The engineers began to plan on a more ambitious scale.

Pierre-Paul de Riquet was one who liked to think big, in fact, huge. He had just started work on the Canal du Midi (twenty years' work and a personal fortune swallowed up, to link the Mediterranean with the Atlantic). What he recommended for Versailles was simple: all they had to do was divert the Loire. His plan started Le Nôtre dreaming: some day soon, great ships from

Orléans or Nantes would be floating out there, opposite his flower beds. In vain did Riquet say, and say again: "That which I have promised, I shall perform. Word of a gentleman." The project was abandoned.

So they decided to harness all the rainwater falling on Saclay Plateau. Miles of small trenches were dug, all leading to the Buc Aquaduct (630 yards long, 50 yards high).

And still the fountains at Versailles clamored for more. Never mind; Louvois proposed that they take on the river Eure. Vauban was summoned, for this was going to be a battle, against the forces of nature and gravity. The river was blocked off. A twenty-five-mile-long trench soon reached all the way to Maintenon. The next job was to cross the valley. Thirty thousand soldiers, commanded by the maréchal d'Uxelles, started construction on the largest aqueduct ever planned: (three miles long, 165 feet high). Swamp fever (six thousand deaths) did not slacken the intense activity of a construction site where ruthless discipline prevailed. Sad to tell, France's enemies took ungentlemanly advantage of the Venice carnival to form an alliance. The troops dropped their spades and departed in haste for the frontiers. To the despair of king, court, and Le Nôtre, the waters of the Eure would never reach Versailles.

That left the Seine. But only if water taken from the river could be raised to the level of the park. The king, as Barbet tells it, "sent criers to every city urging that those who considered themselves expert in matters hydrological display their inventions to Colbert." A gentleman of Liège, Arnold de Ville, came forward. He had heard of a machine devised by a certain Rennequin Sualem, master carpenter. The two engineers were sent for and constructed a scaled-down model below Saint-Germain. The king assembled his court. Soon they were all applauding: the machine had succeeded in lifting water up to the terrace. An order was placed for a veritable monster that would find its way into the history books as "the Marly machine": fourteen wheels, each forty feet in diameter, driving three series of mechanisms,

> to begin with, sixty-four pumps drawing water from the river and directing it against its natural flow into a first-stage reservoir situated on the hillside 159 feet above the Seine. At the second stage, by means of cranks and shafts, the wheels transmitted a back-and-forth motion to two series of rods, not unlike the movement of house bells. The first series of rods, called the little-trestle series, some 656 feet in length, extended up as far as the first reservoir where it drove forty-nine pumps taking water from that reservoir to lift it 185 feet higher, to a second reservoir hollowed out on the crest of the hill. This second reservoir received the second series of rods, called the big-trestle series, 2,133 feet long, driven, like the first series, in a back-and-forth motion, which it transmitted via beams, firstly, halfway up the slope, to the shafts

of thirty pumps that, like the forty-nine previously mentioned, raised the water from the
halfway sump to the upper sump, then, on reaching this latter sump, to the shafts of seventy-eight
pumps that carried the water 188 feet higher still,
to the top of the famous Louveciennes aqueduct.[15]

The engineers had not exactly opted for simplicity! Baron de
Ville lamented that only Vauban understood the mechanism in detail. They came from all over Europe to admire the wonder, with
their hands over their ears, mind you, for the most appalling din
now deafened Bougival Hill. But the goal had been attained: water
in quantity was flowing into the Montbauron Reservoir, 2,600
cubic yards every day.

Those unlucky Versailles fountains! They would not long be
satisfied. Scarcely was construction complete when the king changed
obsessions. He was now entirely preoccupied with his new château.
Water from the machine went to feed their rival fountains in Marly.

* * *

Artists, craftsmen, engineers—our categories and hierarchies were
not known in the seventeenth century. Fountain makers, for instance, had to combine drafting and sculpture, art and technology.
From 1598 to 1784, the fountaineers' guild was controlled by a clan,
les Francine, the Francinis.[16]

Thomas Francini, a twenty-seven-year-old Florentine, was in the employ of the grand duke of Tuscany when his patron received from Henri IV a request for the young man's services. The king having been informed that Francini excelled at grottoes formed of *rocaille* (rustic rockwork) and peopled with hydraulic automatons, wished

to put him in charge of development at Saint-Germain-en-Laye. The air of France seemed to agree with Thomas: he had eleven children, including François and Pierre who became Le Nôtre's accomplices and allies, his permanent representatives. They occupied adjoining houses in Versailles (numbers 16 and 18 on what is now rue Hoche).

The daily life of François de Francine (the French line had been approved for noble status as far back as 1608) cannot fail to surprise us, so attached are we to classifications, specializations, professionalizations, and so forth. He held the position of "maréchal de bataille" in the city of Paris. The duties attending this not entirely honorific post included supervision of police operations. But his main task lay elsewhere. As "General Intendant of the Waterworks and Fountains of France," he planned and executed all water-based entertainments. These quickly proliferated, and the king's pleasure increased in proportion. In the thick of a military campaign, he wrote to Colbert, "I shall be most pleased on my arrival to find Versailles in the state that you describe. Above all look to the pumps; if the new one can cast a 120-inch jet of water, that will be wonderful indeed."

And in 1672 Colbert decreed a detailed set of regulations for each of the fountains:

> Whensoever His Majesty comes forth from the castle, the master fountaineer shall not fail to hold himself in readiness to receive the order, and if His Majesty command that the fountains play, he shall on the instant, with blowing of his whistle, signal for the water to be set running
>
> at les Couronnes,
> at la Pyramide,
> at l'Allée d'eau,
> at le Dragon,
> at la Cérès,
> at le Dosme,
> at l'Apollon,
> at les pieds des chevaux,
> at la Latone,

at les Aigrettes,

at les Bosquets,

and at les Cinq jets.

The fountaineer's lad who is at la Pyramide shall also see to it that when the King has gone by and is out of sight, no more flow is kept up at that place than shall be needed to stir the sheet of water.

It is His Majesty's wish that the same shall be observed whenever some person of consequence is in the park, that is, la Pyramide must play in its fullest beauty, for such time as that person shall be able to see it.

The Dolphins and the Conch shells must be allowed to play at all times and le Dragon must be adapted to the flow of la Pyramide.

As the fountain of le Pavillon can only play if la Pyramide is stopped, the fountaineer's lad responsible for those two fountains shall be mindful never to stop la Pyramide until such time as His Majesty shall have turned into the little avenue of le Pavillon and shall no longer be able to see la Pyramide, at which time the lad shall at once start the water for le Pavillon, so that it is playing before His Majesty can see it.

(And so on and so on: the rules cover ten pages and provide for all the various ways Louis XIV might go when he took a walk.)

* * *

Thus, even the briefest stroll became a spectacle. Wherever the king turned his steps, the fountains performed their carefully rehearsed dances and their songs, too—the entire range of lapping, gurgling, murmuring, and roaring. As he walked among these living waters, His Majesty, who was so fond of the dance, could fancy himself one of the characters in a ballet that had no end.

Le Nôtre being our subject, we are of necessity giving the eyes such precedence of place that the ears are being neglected. But in fact there was singing and playing all around. Every grove of trees had its hidden orchestra, every outdoor collation its serenade. Here, the next day's opera was being rehearsed; there, viols were being tuned.

Turn on the sound, give ear. Versailles was not as we know it today, this huge silent film, congealed in icy silence. If you're short on imagination, listen to the fountains, sole vestige of the music of long ago.

XIII

MATHEMATICAL HAPPINESS

L et w be the width and l the length of a rectangle.

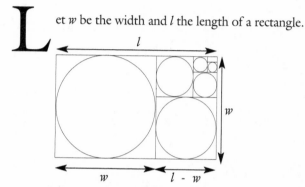

If the rectangle meets the following condition:

$$\frac{l}{w} = \frac{w}{l-w}$$

then this ratio will be present also in the rectangle obtained by subtracting a square from the initial rectangle.

Let us suppose that $w = 1$

and $l = 1 + x$

then $\dfrac{1 + x}{1} = \dfrac{1}{1 + x - 1}$

$x^2 + x - 1 = 0$

$x = \dfrac{-1 + \sqrt{5}}{2}$

$$x \approx 0.62$$

If we add 1

$$n = 1 + x = 1.62$$

What possible satisfaction, I hear you ask, is to be found in these elementary mathematical exercises? And yet, many a mortal joy has derived from those three little figures with the period after the first digit, for what we have here is nothing less than the *golden number.*

Our human eye is rather conservative. It likes things that are identical to other things. Failing that, it seeks responsive chords, re-semblances. That is why the eye treasures anything square; it finds reassurance in that perfect geometric shape. And, faced with a great variety of shapes, the eye again tends to seek out that which is square, or proportions suggesting squareness. The golden ratio serves this function: it prolongs harmony, the harmony that, once perceived, leaves the beholder to mourn its loss forever.

* * *

This almost mystical love of numbers goes far back in time, proba-bly to the sixth century B.C.

Pythagoras was born on Samos, in Asia Minor, whence he emi-grated to Sicily. He was the first to "raise arithmetic above the needs of merchants." Not content with discovering a few fundamental the-orems, he created a kind of religion based on a simple tenet: beneath its seeming disorder, the world is mathematical. Whosoever follows the teachings of science gains access to the divine and simultaneously discovers the laws best suited to the commonweal. "Numbers are the root and wellspring of all things," as one of his disciples said. "Thus, the *tetraktys,* the sum of the first four numbers, represented by the decadic triangle and embracing the natures of both even and odd, will be considered the foundation stone for all of reality" (D. Saintillan). The universe properly understood is governed by harmony and proportion.

All gardeners, though they may not belong to the Pythagorean sect (whose adherents clad themselves in white, shunned houses where someone had died and contact with women in labor, and would not eat broad beans or eggs . . .), share this vision of a harmonious order waiting to be found underneath Earth's depressing chaos. In his *Grammaire des jardins,* the old Belgian master gardener René Pechère, citing many examples to support his contention, demonstrates that "perfect centering" must conform to an angle of 22°.

* * *

Reared in the gentle ways of perspective, Le Nôtre knew every bit of this age-old lore. Since he kept abreast of contemporary science and technology, and spent his life among engineers, he could incorporate into his work all the latest discoveries, notably the arithmetic of series that governs the progression of magnitudes.

As he left no written record, or real notes, or precise plans, or memoirs, his successors have inherited the task of reestablishing the numbers and ratios he must have used.

So it comes about that for three centuries, visitors to Versailles or Vaux have been bemused to see apparently rational, serious men clutching tape measures, protractors, or telescopic sights, walking this way and that over the grounds. They take a measurement and utter an exclamation. They are like children on Easter morning, hunting for the gaily colored eggs that the grown-ups have hidden.

The first of these pursuers of the magic number was Antoine-Joseph Dézallier d'Argenville. His book *La Théorie et la pratique du jardinage* (1709), the standard reference for classical gardens, is chock full of rules that include exact figures:

> Care must be taken to ensure that stairways and perrons rise very gently and do not have many steps: of these there must be an uneven number and there should be no flight exceeding 11 or 13 steps without a landing or resting place two paces in width and the same length as the perron. Each step may have a tread of 15 or 16 inches for a rise of 5 or 6 inches, including the three lines of slope that each step must have for draining off water that would otherwise rot the lap joints . . .

Not all the secrets have been pierced; landscape gardeners continue to measure layouts and angles, hoping they can force the park to confess how it was planned.[17] It reminds one of those ethnologists cut off for years in a jungle where they have been trying to work out indigenous family relationships on a graph. The quest for underlying structure at Versailles is just as difficult, give or take the piranhas and trapdoor spiders. At one location the golden section is applicable; at another, Le Nôtre shakes free of it, in response to this or that constraint imposed by the site. And perhaps a part of our enjoyment derives from the unceasing negotiations between geometry and geography, between order and sudden escape, between the intoxication of control and the delight of letting go.

In the seeming silence of the gardens, a person who has eyes to see can revel in these great unspoken dualisms.

Take, for instance, the two stairways of one hundred steps, that flank the Orangerie, providing a link between the south terrace and the pool of les Suisses. Le Nôtre was involved in their design. What could be more strictly regular than all these neatly piled-up steps? Turn your body a bit and look at it from an angle. Thanks to the overall plan, and the arrangement of the landings, your impression now is one of soft lines gently caressing your eyes.

This was just one example; Versailles abounds in viewer-friendly gestures: the way walls are positioned, the way trees are aligned, the segments of sky or water left unobstructed among clumps of tall trees. Which is why any walk at Versailles is a peaceful pursuit of happiness.

XIV

On *Bonhomie*

The word *bonhomie* has disappeared and with it perhaps even the cluster of qualities its three syllables brought together: kindness; trust (at the risk of being deceived); simplicity, which is apt to be taken for naïveté; and peaceable familiarity with nature. Under the ancien régime, if you wished to suggest the image of a country fellow, a typical country fellow, you used the phrase *"Jacques Bonhomme."*

The most famous *bonhomme* in our history was a minor special officer in the royal forestry administration, Jean de La Fontaine. The *bonhomme* nickname had been bestowed on him by his friends Molière, Racine, and Boileau. If the literary chroniclers are to be believed, his sobriquet had been inspired by affection and exasperation combined: it was impossible to have a sustained conversation with La Fontaine. He would suddenly shut up shop and mentally make good his escape into remote, free-living rural regions whence nothing, not even the loudest music, could bring him back. His abstraction on these occasions gave him a foolish look that elicited jokes and banter. Countless fits were recorded, of this malady born of boredom and called absentmindedness. On one occasion, so the story went, he emerged abruptly from a daydream induced by a wordy lecture on Saint Augustine to ask the theologian whether quite frankly he did not prefer Rabelais. Another time, in the middle of a walk along the Cours-la-Reine, he was reported to have sat down on a bench and stayed there until evening, oblivious to rain and to the inquiries of his friends, immersed as he was in a labor at once absorbing and invisible, perhaps an extended walk in the land of "long-handled herons" or "crows perched upon a tree," as in his fables.

There was no such escapism in Le Nôtre's makeup. Nor could he have so indulged himself. From morn till night this tireless contractor was surrounded by hundreds, nay, thousands of gardeners, construction workers, fountaineers, engineers, mole catchers, tree nurserymen . . . , crowding close, refusing to go away, forever wanting his instructions. There were weeks that saw 36,000 workmen, representing every trade, laboring together on the site at Versailles. Le Nôtre had an army to command. And let it not be forgotten that he was, in addition, "Superintendent of the King's Buildings." Anything less absentminded than that kind of government official would be hard to imagine. From a wall threatening to crumble in ruins at the Luxembourg to a rainspout with a hole in it at Trianon, he was ceaselessly inspecting, supervising, taking note, reprimanding.

Naïveté was not his specialty either. He pursued his career and enlarged his fortune with unmatched virtuosity. Other men, exhausted by this multiplicity of tasks or dazzled by their own glory, might neglect to accumulate worldly goods. Not he. The others, all the others, even Le Brun, even Racine, after enjoying the extreme of royal favor, suffered the extreme of royal coldness, or even a falling-out leading to dismissal. Not he. Over a period of thirty-nine years, not the smallest cloud came between him and the Sun. Anyone who has had some experience of contact with the great and mighty, who has ventured for a few years to steer a course in the treacherous waters of palaces, who has come to know the weather trends prevailing in those intemperate zones (they are like Patagonia, where calms are just the prelude to storms), who has dealt with uncontrolled fits of impatience and the whims of passing moods, such a one can only applaud long and loud the perfect career path of our master gardener. Beneath his unpolished exterior, he was a better courtier than any of them, guiding his little boat successfully through the shoals of royal demands without sacrificing one shred of his genius.

All the evidence points to Le Nôtre's fundamental kindness, his unruffled disposition, his unfailing sense of humor, his spontaneity, his lack of pretension . . . All the human qualities of a *bonhomme* are present. But was he a *bonhomme* by profession?

Even if gardening is one of the agricultural arts, it must be admitted that this man's way of being just a country fellow was like none seen before or since. He was more of a grand-scale developer than a farmer; he was more obsessed with perspective than in love with botany; in his relationship to nature he was the master whose will must always dominate. He imposed on her a rational intelligence that tolerated no deviation. Surprises there might be (in fact there are many), but they were planned, deliberate, meticulous. Chance was banished, order prevailed, the life force was told to toe the line. The park at Versailles makes Japanese visitors think of a giant bonsai; other viewers actually sense hatred in the regimentation of plants and trees.

Certainly nothing about Le Nôtre suggests Saint Francis of Assisi. He did not greet creation with renewed wonder each day, for he was strictly in the business of re-creation. He carried on no dialogue with the birds, but rather with the armies of humans aiding and abetting him as he reshaped the world. Even if the excuse was "masterpiece in progress," to hold nature in such thralldom hardly qualifies as *bonhomie*.

To be truthful, he was a *bonhomme* solely when in the presence of his beloved expanses of water, his parterres, or canals. Only then did he abandon himself to contemplation of a show about which he knew nothing in advance. He had set the stage, now it was up to others: the actor (the sky) and the dancers (the clouds). In the countryside, for instance around La Fontaine's hometown of Château-Thierry, nature was loved for herself. In the city—and though he was a gardener, Le Nôtre, child of the Tuileries, which is to say child of Paris, was a town mouse—the seventeenth century preferred life that was bound by codes. Or reflected in water.

* * *

Bonhomie and tyranny—even tyranny over plants—make an ill-matched couple; *bonhomie* and skill, on the other hand, go well together. When it came to skill, Le Nôtre was a master courtier who could have taught a few tricks to the experts. That includes Baldassare Castiglione, the man who wrote *Il Cortegiano* (the Book of the Courtier), one of sixteenth-century Europe's best-sellers.

Rule number one, from which all the others flow: know your place and stay in it. A man of the soil you are, a man of the soil you remain, no matter what honors have come your way. Saint-Simon unerringly detected compliance with the rule; the little duke hated everybody, but he liked Le Nôtre. The duke was a stickler for rank, a talmudist of hierarchy, and our gardener was a man after his own heart, a man who kept in mind the rank conferred on him by his birth and sought no other, however much he excelled at his job. People like Le Nôtre were the pillars of a social system threatened by arrivistes and encroachers. "Never did he step outside his condition or forget himself": for Saint-Simon no epitaph could bestow higher praise. Ten words said it all and described the ideal society: one that never changes.

The fellow, the *bonhomme,* understood perfectly. How, day after day, could he get the pack of jealous hounds that made up the royal court to stop snapping at his heels? By offering them what they would find reassuring: modesty and unpretentious behavior. "Fear not, ye princes of the blood, ye envious countesses, I may share private moments with the king, I may have turned Île-de-France on its ear and created the most stunning garden in the world, I'm still nothing but a poor country fellow, and beg to remain your lordships' most humble and respectful servant (etc., etc.)." At which their lordships puffed out their chests: "Decent chap, that Le Nôtre fellow! Talented, of course, but shows respect for his betters!" And presto! The deed was done. Our friend could go about his work. For persuading those in higher places to let you do your job in peace, nothing beats telling them over and over what they like to hear you say.

Came 1675. The king decided to ennoble him. It was an honor, of course, but a danger, too: what reaction could he expect from the gang of aristocrats whom he had been so careful not to stir up all this time and who would now suddenly see a gauntlet flung down right in the heart of their exclusive domain? Le Nôtre got himself out of the trap in his usual fashion, that is, by remembering his place. Me, with a coat of arms, Sire? "Very well, then, three snails crowned with a cabbage heart. And how could I possibly leave out my spade? Don't I have my spade to thank for the signal honor Your Majesty is conferring upon me?" Versailles roared with laughter and was deeply touched. How could anybody possibly resent this gem of a man? Le Nôtre was now the possessor of a title, and nobody's feelings had been hurt and nobody had been disowned. "On a field sable with one chevron or accompanied by three snails argent, the two on the chief addorsed and the one on the point turned toward the left."

* * *

Here, then, was a man who, to all appearances, had not an enemy in the world . . . What sort of person was he, really? We all know how individuals that are too well liked attract negative comment: they must be spineless creatures, shameless flatterers, all charm and no depth . . . Either they are utterly lazy and will not put much effort into any cause, not even into quarrels, or else they are immensely hardworking and have grown themselves a set of duck feathers: no rain gets through, they are impervious, as long as nothing interferes with what they're working on. Obviously, Le Nôtre belonged to the second group. He was too busy to worry about who might be scoffing behind his back or maneuvering to get him sidelined. He made his way. He laid out his avenues and paths. The duels *he* fought were those of the creative artist: every waking day he had to contend with facile solutions, needless repetition, servile acquies-cence, phony posturing, all the sluggish promptings of the mind. Against these foes he pitted his strength and his honor. Where other matters were concerned, he let tongues wag, smiled, and fell back on his favorite tactic, playing the uncouth lout. A rather unlikely lout, if you stop to think about it, one who had frequented court circles since childhood (at the Tuileries), as had his father before him . . .

* * *

The harder you try to assemble those few facts known about him so as to form an idea of the real Le Nôtre, the more layers peel away from our storybook picture of the good, kind gardener with the muddy clothes, always trotting along beside the king of kings with his spade over his shoulder, and saying whatever came to mind.

Extreme contradictions coexisted in his mental makeup. This unassuming man was a creative force, a demiurge. This man who showed decent respect (for social rank) was dictatorial (when it came to landscapes). His frank, open manner had a strong element of country cunning; his unaffected ways were highly sophisticated.

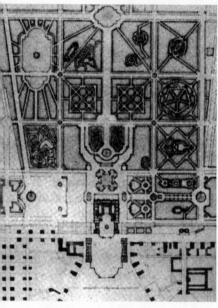

You are supposed to think he was simple and straightforward; you are likewise supposed to think the gardens he created are simple and straightforward. It's a trap . . . which only catches visitors who are lazy. Others will take time to look carefully around; those are the visitors who realize that *bonhomie* is an old-fashioned world, worth going out of your way to explore.

L ike all creators, Le Nôtre often ceased to believe that anything existed outside his own creations. In his eyes, Paris
had disappeared, as had the surrounding segments of countryside,
fields, churches, even fortified hilltop castles. The visible world was
reduced to the gardens of his begetting: islands standing out from
the sea. A great many islands, for by now commissions were coming
thick and fast. Every wealthy man, every man of power wanted his
estates to boast a work by Le Nôtre. It was a way of flattering the king
and sharing his tastes. The master designer inspected his islands repeatedly, for nothing sinks out of sight faster than an abandoned park.

This archipelago of gardens[18] had its flagship: Versailles. Le
Nôtre could never set foot on that particular island without experi-
encing a sense of pride. And pride is no mean pleasure. But other
destinations brought private satisfactions of a more personal kind.
The salient point is that each port of call made him happy in its own
special fashion, and variety is what gives an archipelago its charm:
you travel to the next island without having to say farewell to the island you are leaving.

* *
*

A Terrace at Saint-Germain

A free gift, a fit of anger, and a victory.

Usually, Le Nôtre had to resort to trickery in his dealings with terrain, and labor mightily to produce commanding views. In Saint-Germain, acting over thousands of years, geography had done all the work for him. Facing the old castle, which held such bad childhood memories for Louis XIV, a long avenue (a thousand *toises,* a mile and a quarter in today's measures) dominates the valley of the Seine from a great height. After a rain, when the skies are clearest, the eye can see all the way to Paris. For once, there was no need to assemble thousands of workmen: admission to the show was free.

But a retaining wall had collapsed. In what manner was the terrace to be rebuilt? Architect Le Vau had one response: his schema called for a straight line. Le Nôtre had another; his concept was different. The gardener never behaved again as he behaved now. This normally gentle, meek, accommodating man suddenly became enraged, unyielding, and irascible. He even went so far as threatening to resign. Eventually he won the day. A note scribbled on a plan describes the terrible battle; the note is written in his own hand and couched in his own special style:

> Plan that was made for the terrace and over which
> Mr. Le Vau argued with me that Mr. Colbert, too,
> did not want it done as it now is. But in the end he
> granted it me after arguing hard that he would rue
> the day and sent it back to me refusing to do it.

The layout that was adopted involved a slight deviation in the line of the avenue, curving it inward toward the forest. The result was three additional pleasures for the eye: the avenue took on added life and the foliage added depth, while a portion of that lovely wall supporting the whole structure was now visible. This imperceptible break sums up Le Nôtre's genius. To a domain that seemed straight-lined and cold, he brought softness and surprise. With a tiny touch, he highlighted the garden's two main functions: to be decorative and to prompt further scrutiny. A garden embellishes a landscape, but at the same time offers new perspectives onto that landscape.[19]

* * *

Pure Geometry at Fontainebleau

Like Saint-Germain, Fontainebleau had long been an abode of the court, with royal sojourns as far back as Francis I. Each successive monarch imposed his architectural contribution and his ideas. What between additions and corrections, the garden was no longer too sure what message it was trying to convey. When he arrived on the scene, Le Nôtre at once began organizing and simplifying.

The pride of Fontainebleau was its "Tiber garden," a giant open space (ten acres), with no visual relief or adornment except for the arabesques of its embroidery-style beds. To fill this somewhat over-powering space, Le Nôtre decided on abstract composition, unfet-tered and unapologetic. He invented a design based on squares: the first four, each with a scoop out of one corner, surrounded the fifth, an ornamental pool. The very quintessence of the "French-style garden." Geometricians thought this Euclidean promenade was just grand. Humans with more normal tastes hastened onward to the less radical places in the park, where nature, under careful supervision, of course, recovered at least some of her prerogatives.

* * *

Dawn at Sceaux

Colbert had just acquired a piece of property and, like everyone else, was desirous of having Le Nôtre design his park. But he was haunted by the memory of Vaux. He wanted the land developed in a manner befitting his rank, yet he feared lest too magnificent a display provoke the king's wrath. The gardener did not need to have Colbert's dual concern spelled out for him and, spurred on by these constraints, achieved a masterpiece of controlled design. Water was there in all its forms: showering, cascading, or simply dormant; avenues wider than any yet seen; grassy sweeps; rows of poplars as a gesture to Italy. It was a work of breadth, proud in the service of a master, exactly like the minister himself. And, that none might miss the significance and go carrying tales to Louis XIV, owner and artist voiced loud and clear, to every willing listener, the symbolic value of the canal: it went toward the east, where Sceaux's Aurora Pavillion lay. Aurora was Colbert himself, clearing a path for the Sun.

* * *

The Flowers at Trianon

The need for a secondary residence affects kings as it does bourgeois: work on Versailles had barely begun when Louis XIV wanted a place where he could get away from it and bring a few intimates together in peace and quiet. And so was born a first version of Trianon, the "porcelain" Trianon, created by Le Vau and d'Orbay, to be replaced twenty years later with a more ambitious grouping designed by Robert de Cotte and Hardouin-Mansart. This was where flowers had their realm. The king liked his flowers to smell strong and change often. Le Nôtre grew them in countless sandstone pots that he buried in the flower beds. As there was no shortage of labor, all he had to do was replace the pots and the garden was instantly transformed. Tulips, hyacinth, daffodils, narcissus . . . The most exotic species and those most susceptible to cold were not forgotten: they were grown under glass, trotted out for the day, put back inside for the night. And the king said bravo! There was nothing he enjoyed more than this forcing of his will upon the changing seasons.

* * *

The Challenge of Saint-Cloud

What could have been more unpromising than the demesne belonging to Monsieur, the king's brother? Slopes going every which way, plateaux, little valleys, a site with no overall unity, no perspective other than a meander of the Seine, imparting a triangular shape to the one relatively extensive flat area . . . To top it all, the only obvious spectacle wrought by nature, namely a large waterfall, was already there for people out walking to gawk at, before Le Nôtre arrived . . . Could anything interesting be made of this geographical clutter? Studying the plan for Saint-Cloud is a very instructive exercise for landscape architects: how to imprint an idea on a refractory piece of land. Le Nôtre did not abandon the visual gaps he was so fond of, nor his alleés, his branching pathways or his *ronds-points.* But we must look elsewhere to find the spirit of the place. He had to turn all these incompatibles to advantage, changing them into so many surprises. Accordingly, he included any number of *bosquets,* green bowers, hidden meeting places. And Saint-Cloud owes its charm to all these secret realms, laying siege to a unity you sense but cannot find.

* * *

Garden of Mirrors at Chantilly

Along with alcohol and religion, the penchant for things botanical is a refuge much favored by those possessed of strong emotions and who have suffered disappointment. The pursuit of plant life offers gentle consolation for battles lost in love or politics. How often we find yesterday's sex kitten trying to appease the flame still burning within her by grafting and layering! How many ex-presidents prune furiously away at their rosebushes as they foment bloody returns to power! In the days of the Fronde, le Grand Condé had come within an inch of seizing the reins of government. Returning willy-nilly to conformity and obedience, he devoted his energies to his lands.

The château, inherited from the Montmorency family, was an odd creature: a triangular heap of heterogeneous parts, a Renaissance structure on feudal foundations. It could not be turned into an aesthetic focal point. Le Nôtre appended a terrace to serve that function. It is amusing to imagine the artist's secret satisfaction, his hidden feeling of revenge. At last, a garden not playing second fiddle to its château! At last, glory goes to the terrace, whence the gaze radiates out.

And water, water, everywhere.

Still waters, cut out into ornamental ponds of every shape.

Waters kept ceaselessly moving by fountains and jets.

Running waters: the Nonette, the local river, coming from Senlis and cascading down, before flowing slowly away as a canal of noble proportions, over a course two miles in length.

The result was that here if anywhere the comparison with an archipelago can be sustained. Parterres here seemed to be islands in the embrace of all those aqueous expanses. And whenever the wind dropped, and the watery surfaces ceased to be blurred by even the slightest breeze, you would have sworn that Chantilly was afloat 'twixt land and sky.

And this, Versailles notwithstanding, was Le Nôtre's favorite child.

* * *

West of Trianon,
an Act of Repentance, or a Premonition

For the king of Sweden's architect, who had come to study the achievements of French creative builders, Le Nôtre penned in 1693 this description of a secret little enclosure dear to his heart:

> The springs run . . . hidden by undergrowth
> lengthwise and widthwise, a woods of standing
> timber covering the whole, the trees being well
> separated, which meant we could build little
> canals that wind along following no pattern and
> come out in the open spaces around the trees,
> with fountains located irregularly here and there,
> and all the canals diverge and connect up, flowing
> one into the next on account of a slope too gentle
> to notice. On either side in the woods are two
> runnels falling in small sheets of water and in
> these, fountains throwing jets twelve feet high
> ending up in two water chasms that disappear

into the ground. I cannot sufficiently describe here the beauty of the place, there is a freshness where the ladies go to do needlework, play, confer on this spot its beauty and distinction by their presence. You come into it directly from the apartment and on the same level. So that from the apartment you may go privily into all the beautiful parts, various alleés, *bosquets,* woods, of the whole garden thus privily; I must tell you that it is the only garden, and the Tuileries also, that I know of for walking contented at one's ease and also the loveliest. I grant those others their beauty and grandeur, but for most ease and contentment.

Thierry Mariage, who discovered the treasure just quoted, has aptly remarked that "it will be odd, to say the least, if we must henceforth consider [Le Nôtre] among the precursors of the picturesque [that is, English] garden."[20]

* * *

A River at Marly

Weary of Trianon, where he had the great palace too close at hand, Louis XIV wanted a retreat devoted to friendship and the hunt. His choice fell on a narrow vale between Versailles and Saint-Germain.

Serious work on the gardens began after 1694, and historians are still arguing over who should be credited with the project's conception. Le Nôtre was not concerned directly; he was now too old to oversee the gigantic construction involved. But there exists in Stockholm an "initial plan for the river," a drawing in his hand, done with pen and ink, wash, black lead, watercolor, and red pencil highlighting.[21]

The work of harnessing and channeling the river lasted thirty-five years, until Louis XIV, financially ruined, decided to replace it with a "great carpet of greenery."

Spat forth by sea monsters, the river splashed its way from the heights of Marly down sixty-three steps of red and green marble.

That drawing is the master's last known sketch.

* * *

Many other islands in Le Nôtre's archipelago could be named: Courances, Clagny, Meudon, Choisy, Dampierre, Issy, Pontchartrain, Champ de Bataille, Montmirail, Navarre, Anet, Montjeu, Castres, and Castries . . . It sounds rather like that song we used to sing as children: "Orléans, Beaugency, Vendôme, Vendôme . . . " Love of country penetrating our very pores in the form of place-names, repeated over and over.

Sometimes he would see personally to every bit of the work; sometimes all he did was bestow a hasty scribble on some landowning family, whose members would piously preserve it. Most often, he was present only in someone's fondest dreams. Legend has him making innumerable trips to every part of Europe. In fact, he never left France except when he went to Italy. There was some basis for all these imaginings, so profoundly had he changed the way the way people looked at things. One has but to visit Joseph I's palace at Schönbrunn (1690), Peter the Great's Peterhof at the entrance to the Gulf of Finland, or Philip V's La Granja, near Segovia, to realize how true that is.

And although he probably never crossed the Channel, it was Le Nôtre who did the first drawings for the garden at Greenwich, east of London, where our planet's time of day has its origin.

XVI.

T R U S T   A N D   B E T R A Y A L

For Le Nôtre, the Tuileries were in a category apart, neither flagship nor one isle in an archipelago. They were home port, secure anchorage. They were the particular place that attended your birth, that taught you all you knew, that felt no fear as you set off on your adventures, secure in the knowledge that to it you would return.

From childhood and until his death, Le Nôtre's home was at the Tuileries. This was where, each time he could be away from the king, he was reunited with his wife. This was the place where his children would start to grow up, and then die.

He had redesigned the Tuileries Gardens in 1666 and never stopped reworking them. He took out the street that lay stupidly separating the palace from its park. He tore up old trees that blocked the view, replacing them with 6,000 hornbeam birches, 8,000 maples, 400 cypress, and as many linden trees, plus 1,500 yews.

Especially, he laid out four avenues, one of which was to become world famous. The first of them started from a point facing the center of the palace and ran right across the gardens. Once past the perimeter wall, it emerged onto a *patte d'oie* intersection, a vast flat space from which an accumulation of unauthorized buildings had been entirely cleared away. The resulting esplanade was destined for glory and renown: it is today's Place de la Concorde. From it, and bordered with elms, radiated the other three allées: to the south, the Cours-la-Reine, which followed the Seine; northward, a promenade that was pushed through toward the faubourg of Le Roule; and in the middle, the "grand avenue of the Tuileries," later lengthened and renamed the Champs-Elysées.

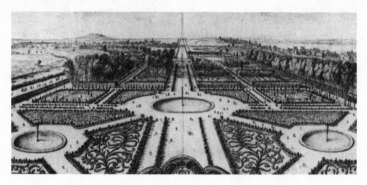

The forest where the king was taught to hunt, and the one-time rabbit warren, and the tangled copses, the dense old masses of foliage where little André had regularly got lost, everything went.

Creative geniuses are wont to display violent behavior when confronted with the scene of their childhood.

* *
  *

Le Nôtre was indebted to Fouquet for Vaux, that is, for his first claim to fame. The superintendent had large trees, yews and pines, around his much-loved house in Saint-Mandé. Le Nôtre was notified of Louis XIV's request that his gardener pull up these trees and replant them, live, in the Tuileries Gardens, complete with the balls of earth around their roots. As Majesty willed, so it was done, without Le Nôtre daring to utter the slightest word, the meekest protest. How long did he secretly harbor his silence and his shame?

Out of the entire coterie that once had gathered about Fouquet, only La Fontaine remained faithful.[22] True, he needed neither fortune nor acres to produce his work. His pen sufficed, his pen plus a few pompous animals that no one could possibly harm.

Men with power often derive pleasure from forcing artists to commit filthy acts of betrayal such as this. It does not prove how deeply attached to them the artist is, but rather that they have succeeded in imprisoning someone's freedom.

A delightful feeling, so I've been told.

XVII

EMBRACING HIS HOLINESS

Master Le Nôtre will be traveling to Italy not so
much to satisfy his curiosity as to look about carefully for anything fine enough to warrant imita-
tion in the Royal Residences, or apt to provide
him new ideas as he daily devises noble plans for
His Majesty's pleasure or satisfaction.

So reads a piece of official correspondence informing the French
ambassador that the king's gardener was about to arrive in Rome.

Le Nôtre had cherished an affection for Italy since his adolescent
years at the Louvre. His mentor Vouet had talked of nothing else:
Italy, said Vouet, was the very homeland of beauty. But our hero had
never been. The years had gone by, each so filled with work, at home
in Île-de-France, that he dared not be away at all, much less consider
crossing the Alps. The best things in Le Nôtre's life did not come
early. For him, happiness was a patient flower, slow to blossom.
When at last Colbert granted him leave, he had passed his sixty-fifth
birthday. This visitor making his first acquaintance with the Eternal
City was almost an old man. Well, perhaps not his very first acquaintance: he had spent so many hours copying drawings and
paintings that were tributes to Rome.

* *
  *

His personal visits there began with someone older yet: Gianlorenzo Bernini, le Cavalier Bernin to the French. He was eighty-one and had a reputation almost on a par with Leonardo's, earned in almost as many fields: sculpture, painting, architecture, decorating, poetry . . . His masterpieces were legion: *The Ecstasy of Saint Teresa,* the baldachin of St. Peter's, his portrait of Urban VIII. Louis XIV had sent for Bernini fifteen years earlier to rebuild the Louvre. The ambition of this Italian genius knew no bounds: "Sire, I have seen the palaces of emperors and popes, and those of sovereign princes . . . For a king of France, a king of the present day, we must build things of greater size, greater splendor . . . I will not undertake anything small." But Colbert wanted rather to build for comfort. So they had sent the genius away, but had compensated and consoled him generously by commissioning a piece of work, an equestrian statue of the king. Time was passing and no statue had appeared. Le Nôtre's mission was to inquire how it was coming along. Tread softly, they had warned him, le Cavalier is a son of Naples and quick to lose his temper.

Bernini was a foxy fellow. He was well aware of his visitor's standing at Versailles. It would be a good idea to enlist the other man's sympathy; then Le Nôtre could be his privileged spokesman in dealings with Louis XIV, possessor of Europe's greatest appetite for construction. Advanced age has never stopped any architect from wanting to go on building. Bernini pointed to a heap of sketches and engravings on his desk, saying he admired them extremely and only wished he knew who they were by. The visitor blushed and stammered; needless to say, they were his work. Le Nôtre had walked into the trap. The Italian had made a friend of him. When the statue finally came, our gardener would defend it with all his might against every adverse opinion . . .

* * *

Pope Innocent XI was another one who loved gardens. Upon being apprised of the Frenchman's presence in Rome, he invited him to the Vatican. Le Nôtre had brought with him Pierre Desgots, his nephew. Desgots was a scholarship student at the Académie de France, founded there in Rome thirteen years earlier, and spoke Italian. After appropriate genuflexions, the guest got back to his feet and conversation began. It went on for hours, enraging the cardinal secretary in charge of papal schedules. The supreme pontiff wanted to know all about Versailles. The waterworks were a special source of amazement; by what miracle could so many canals, fountains, and waterfalls be supplied with water? Le Nôtre explained, drew pictures, and was carried away with excitement: "I can die happy, I have seen the world's two greatest men, Your Holiness and my master the king." Innocent XI slowly waved an old and weary hand: "The king is a great conquering monarch; I am a poor priest, servant of the servants of God." This was too much for Le Nôtre's self-control. As Desgots described it, "his only guide now was his entrails"; he took the pope in his arms and, with his nephew looking on in terror and the cardinal in horror, kissed him.

Proud of his outburst and seeing no harm in it, Le Nôtre wrote a letter to his friend Bontemps, chief personal valet to the king, setting forth all the details. The account was routinely read aloud at the daily ceremonial of His Majesty's rise from slumber. The princesses and dukes in attendance refused to believe it: no human being endowed with the gift of reason would dare kiss the pope on both cheeks. And as the nobility loved gambling, sums began to be wagered on whether such a scene had really taken place. "Stay your betting," said Louis XIV. "Every time I come home from the wars, I, too, am kissed by Le Nôtre."

* * *

Aside from being flattered by a Cavalier and embraced by His Holiness, he does not appear to have enriched his experience at all during the visit to Italy. Though he might be stirred by the churches and sculptures, though he might marvel at one or two of the fountains, the gardens typical of Rome bored him. Lacking in scope, wanting in discipline, repeating age-old patterns without originality . . . It was a major disappointment and cast a shadow over his entire stay. Some journeys, like some loves, come too late. One's own imagination has filled the void left by overlong absence. And reality, even if Italian, struggles for air: dreams have taken up all the space. Someone consulted him about a residence in Camigliano. Le Nôtre suggested reflective water surfaces, his usual solution. His heart wasn't in it. He just wanted to go home.

XVIII.

SLIGHTS

Since a courtier's every expectation is dependent on someone more powerful than he, any life spent at any royal court is one long meal of slights to be swallowed. And every honor, at court, is paid for with commensurate slices of humble pie.

In spite of his best efforts, Le Nôtre could not escape what the cooks served up. In his case the main (though not the only) vile dish to be stomached was called Hardouin; given name, Jules. As a great-nephew of François Mansart (1598–1666), he thought it useful, early in his career, to add that illustrious patronymic to his own, becoming Jules Hardouin-Mansart. He soon made his little device even more effective by shelving the Hardouin altogether and being called simply "Mansart." It worked. Then as now, an uninformed general public mixed the two architects up as one composite person: they were François, the forerunner, a man of genius on a par with Bernini, and inventor of the noble style; and Jules, the follower, a man of talent, whose skill at drawing was equaled by his skill at finding favor with the king.

It was Le Nôtre who brought him into the group at Versailles, in 1675. Once ensconced, he seized power, and not just at the castle.

Before he came, tasks were shared out in such a way that the gardener was left with the garden, thickets of trees included, even if the idea had been sketched out by Le Brun. Hardouin was not a man to be satisfied with inspiring others. He built things, he built them everywhere, and, as he enjoyed the favor of Louis XIV, nothing and no one could stop him.

The golden legend of Versailles would have it that no cloud ever darkened relations between the two artists. How can anyone subscribe to such a myth? How could a mighty creative spirit like Le Nôtre, master in his domain of terraces, allées, water mirrors, and clearings, possibly have accepted the protégé's growing encroachment on his territory and nursed no secret resentment? Naturally he put a good face on it. Naturally he kept his rancor to himself. On no account was he about to smash the *bonhomie* image he had built up right from the first. But surely he felt increasing irritation, as well as regret at having opened the door one fateful day to this shameless young usurper.

Rather than believing this biblical story of idyllic cooperation (this, dearest Jules, is merely my whole life's work; feel free to do whatever you like with it), I prefer to seek the truth from the man who wrote memoirs. Saint-Simon's intuitive flair, even with his added embellishments, brings us closer to deep-seated human weaknesses, which is to say closer to truth.

Hardouin had taken a *bosquet* previously developed by Le Nôtre and turned it into a colonnade, something quite unique be it said, "a peristyle, circular in shape . . . , composed of thirty-two Ionic columns . . . , including eight of violet breccia, twelve of Languedoc marble, and twelve of deep blue marble . . ."

The king called for an opinion on this widely acclaimed piece of work.

"Sire," replied Le Nôtre, "you have turned a mason into a gardener; he has served you a dish prepared in his own special style."

Which shows that a slight acknowledged is a slight already half digested.

XIX

GREAT LOVE

Ordinarily, women are drawn to gardeners. A gardener is so close to nature; he knows such mysterious things—a mystery enhanced in many instances by a sprinkling of Latin terms; he respects the weather, and the seasons, and processes that refuse to be rushed; his job, his whole concern, is to give pleasure: traits bound to attract. Not to mention a number of physical factors that many a fair dame has found disturbing: broad, calloused hands, faces etched by the out-of-doors, the scent of earth and sweat given off when the day has brought rough work . . . And I must not neglect the setting, which lends itself to embraces of an unaccustomed sort: a private space, enclosed by hedges or by a double row of espaliers, gives rise to more fresh ideas than does the connubial bedroom. All sorts of women, in every age and era, have yielded to the charms of the landscaping fraternity.

Thus we might easily have pictured Le Nôtre's life filled with happy encounters: besides his success with plants, he was famous; the most beautiful ladies at court made little cooing noises when he walked by; and it was an age when people needed little persuading. But, in fact, there is nothing to report. Not the slightest hint of impropriety. No woman is known to have crossed his path save the one he was married to, and nothing is known about *her* except that she ran his house with a firm hand and made sure that worldly goods kept accumulating.

And so we are obliged to abandon the petticoats and turn elsewhere in the search for our hero's extramarital passion.

* * *

Anyone totally unfamiliar with the spheres of power imagines a world where self-interest reigns supreme and reigns alone, a world whose inhabitants vie only for place; they would kill their grandmother for advancement. They dream of nothing but dominance, personal glory, and the acquisition of wealth. It is assumed that when they have satisfied these cravings, they sit in the silence of their offices, rapt in boundless, solitary enjoyment—the onanism of the ambitious.

Anyone totally unfamiliar with the world of power does not know the infinite capacities for devotion that sometimes emerge in high places. Nor has the uninitiated any idea of the force and variety of *feelings* that convulse even the most hardened among coldblooded monsters. Love and hate are more common currency in those corridors than calculation and manipulation. A harsher than usual word from the prince, a small compliment, a sudden coolness or some imperceptible mark of esteem, and hearts begin to beat wildly, cheeks are suffused by blushes or go white as a sheet, brows run with sweat and palms are suddenly moist. Behind their austere facades, palaces echo to the lament of painful passions. The souls of the mighty in their council chamber are as tormented as the hearts of schoolgirls in their dormitory. As with all administrations, idyllic relationships between colleagues do spring up. But true torches burn only for the person in charge, especially if what he's in charge of is the country. That individual, as I can testify, casts a spell no one, not even—in the case of France—those among us most imbued with secularism and republicanism, can ward off. This being so, how must people have felt in the mid-seventeenth century if they had access to the king, the anointed of God himself and also the incarnation of a France going back twelve hundred years?

Playwright Jean Racine exemplifies this worship. From 1664 to 1677, from *Andromaque* to *Phèdre* by way of *Bérénice* and *Iphigénie,* he spent thirteen years probing the human soul, and they were thirteen years of masterpieces, thirteen years of successes. No matter. Louis XIV had but to appoint him royal historiographer for Racine to walk away from theater without a backward glance and devote himself to his great love, the only passion that counted. From then on, all he cared about were his *privances,* the word used by Saint-Simon when referring to his own private moments with the king. Addressing the Académie on 2 January 1685, Racine described what was his ultimate dream:

> To study him [the king] in the most trivial actions
> of his life, no less great, no less a hero, no less ad-
> mirable, a fount of equity, a fount of humanity, al-
> ways at peace, always the master of his passions,
> with no unevenness of temper, no weakness, in a
> word the wisest and most perfect of men.[23]

And when, in 1698, Mme. de Maintenon gave him the cold shoulder, Racine thought he would surely die. If the royal consort was shutting him out, he had lost the king. His twenty years of service, his thousands of flattery-filled pages and apologia-filled verses, his hundreds of days playing soldier in mud and rain, the bigoted dramas (*Esther* and *Athalie*) he had produced to order, it would all have been to no purpose. His mental anguish was the death of him. "Such deep chagrin did he conceive from these events, that he fell into a melancholy and lived not two years after" (Saint-Simon).

* * *

Le Nôtre may have been a man of fewer words than Racine, but his passion was no less great. And he had better luck: he was continually at the king's side. Indeed Louis set far more store by his park than by the monument of praises erected by that sometime second-rate dramatist. And Versailles was permanently under construction. For some thirty-five years, the monarch and his gardener laid their heads together over plans and drawings, strode side by side along the allées, interminably argued trees and parterres, stopped, when evening had come, at the edge of one of the terraces and silently gazed at the vistas that together they had opened up.

Colbert was another person the king could expect to see on a daily basis. But his conversation and his field of reference were of a drier sort, and besides, he died in 1683. Other representatives of the arts, Molière, Lully, received commissions for works, were duly applauded, and went on their way. Their contact did not begin to compare with the priceless gift of His Majesty's presence, every waking day when Majesty was not defending the realm at one of its borders. Le Nôtre's only possible competition, for the privilege he enjoyed, was from women, but until Mme. de Maintenon, women—including Montespan—came and went. The gardener remained. Not one of His Majesty's other subjects enjoyed similar *privances*. Not one stayed so permanently lodged in the heart of His Majesty's affections. With no one else did Louis XIV walk life's path, or engage in converse, to the extent he did with Le Nôtre.

Often, at Versailles, I prick up my ears, hoping to recapture the conversation, a-third-of-a-century long, between that most puissant of monarchs, the Sun made flesh, to whose will all things, even the weather, must bend, and that man of the soil, changing with the seasons, who always worked *with* Nature, even though he forced her compliance as no one had done before. I can hear them talking . . . on every imaginable subject, or none at all, as they walk along: "I find this grove enchanting, I'm worried about my son, how are my fountains doing? The Dutch war, just smell those linden blossoms.

That Louvois fellow is a pest, do you get heartburn when you've eaten game? There's no end to those wretched moles . . ."

After summer, comes fall. And then it's spring again. And still they walk. The court watches and wonders. What can they find to talk about after all this time? Two inseparables; along the canal or emerging from an arbor. They're walking through their dream: the park they have both created. There are days when I think Versailles is just the mark of their footsteps reaching down to us across the years.

* * *

Of La Fontaine's couple the Grasshopper and the Ant, Le Nôtre favored the ant. He liked to store up and collect. Nevertheless, in 1693 he made the king a gift of the best he had: sculptures, vases, and, especially, thirty-one paintings, including three Poussins (*The Adulteress, The Baptism of Saint John,* and *Moses Rescued from the Waters*), a Domenichino (*Adam and Eve Driven Forth from Paradise*), and two Claude Lorrains (*Landscape* and *Seaport*). A delighted Louis XIV hung them in the royal apartments . . . and rewarded the giver with a pension of six thousand livres.

Giving to the king in order to get from him may strike us as a strange practice, smacking more of self-interest than of generosity. The century did not look at it in that light. What mattered was the king, not the money. For him to accept a present from you was a mark of esteem (he had turned down Vaux, which Fouquet was offering him). And the resulting gratuity was an index of his pleasure and goodwill. Everyone at court came to admire the gift; admiration for Le Nôtre increased tenfold as a result. Here, beyond a doubt, was a man who knew how to endear himself to the king.

* * *

As time passed, however, a source of friction was arising and spoiling their friendship. To put it succinctly, Louis XIV now considered himself a gardener. Had he not spent years walking, looking, discussing, commanding? Had La Quintinie not given him (a few) lessons in pruning and grafting? His Majesty believed that he now fully possessed the science of botany and the art of layout. The hour had struck, so His Majesty felt, and he was now ready to bring forth wonders all by himself.

Le Nôtre's nephew Claude Desgots has left this first-rate account of a monarch in the grip of creative fervor, with the professional practitioner, one part ruffled feathers, one part sardonic superiority, looking on:

> Although Louis XIV did not abate his admiration
> of Le Nostre's rare gift for gardening, that great
> Prince yet wanted to see the birth of gardens
> whose charms he would owe to none but himself.
> Le Nostre was at this time eighty years old: his
> long frequentation of Court had failed to quench
> in him a love for truth: he did not consider that

the greatest King in the world had so perfect a
grasp of garden arts as did his gardener, and said
as much without holding back: for some while he
disputed; but being desirous, he said, of setting a
distance between life and death, he resolved to re-
tire and asked the King for permission so to do.

Permission granted, not without regrets expressed time and time
again, and assurances of continued affection. Also various kindly
gestures, some of them monetary.

* * *

When shared labors have ceased to nourish them, many friendships
die, but this one persisted.

It couldn't die. There were too many ties binding the king and
his gardener, starting with one unshakeable certainty: both of them
knew in their inmost being that they had taken a very unlikely location and together turned it into a work of peerless perfection. Only
the Manchu emperors, at the other end of the planet, had dared to
undertake construction of so ambitious a garden, where heaven and
earth join to sing of the god-monarch in his glory. But our two
Frenchmen, king and gardener, knew nothing about China; hence,
judged in terms of ambition and success, they believed they were
unique. This privately shared belief was the strongest of bonds.

Each, moreover, admitted what he owed the other.

Without the king, Molière's greatness would still have shone for ever and ever. If not for the king, if not for the fateful encounter that redirected his talent to hagiography, where it petrified, Racine would not have abandoned the theater so young (he was thirty-eight). But the art that gardeners practice is more dependent. Had it not been for the king, Le Nôtre would have joined the ranks of the Mollets, Bouchards, and Desgots, and the like, the army of creators whose greatest dreams never get past the drawing-board.

As for Louis, he was the king. And the very notion of suggesting he had a friend, that is, an equal of sorts, was an attack on the royal person and warranted the Bastille. But again . . . What remains of his years as king, other than Versailles? And what would Versailles be, without its grounds? The great and powerful, who already have everything life can offer, have just one thing they can look forward to: immortality. Trust them to put as much skill and tenacity into arranging for that, as they did into achieving power. Every time he saw a bent, aging, crippled Le Nôtre coming toward him, Louis secretly gave thanks. Soon their difference in age would become irrelevant. Soon death would have swallowed both of

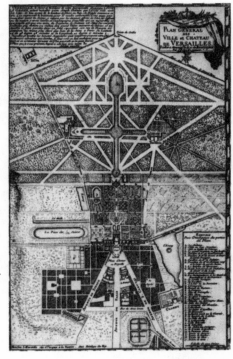

them. And the only traces they would leave behind would be called Grand Canal, Trianon, Latona Terrace, or Neptune Basin.

* * *

Le Nôtre continued to pay frequent visits to the king at various royal residences. One spring afternoon, the old man arrived at Marly and expressed his surprise. The previous autumn, there had been only meadow and arable land. Now, six months later, there were groves and dense woods. No one, before Louis XIV, had ever undertaken the transplanting of thirty-year-old trees on such a scale. "For twenty leagues round about," Desgots tells us, "he denuded the countryside of chestnut and linden trees."

Louis XIV explained: "The outlay is great, but the pleasure is immediate. Past a certain age, the gardens one plants will no longer be for oneself, unless such measures are taken."

And he invited Le Nôtre to come for a drive in these new forests of his. His Majesty, Desgots continues,

> climbed into his covered chaise drawn by mem-
> bers of his Swiss regiment, and gave orders that
> the venerable old man be seated in another very
> similar conveyance. You can readily imagine how
> touched a loyal subject, sincerely devoted to his
> master, must have been by so distinguishing an
> act of kindness. Le Nostre, with tears in his eyes,
> finding himself beside the King, and perceiving

the superintendent of buildings, Mr. Mansart, who was following on foot, exclaimed: "In very truth, sire, the *bonhomme* who was my father would stare to see me in a carriage alongside the greatest King of them all: it cannot be denied that Your Majesty uses his Mason and his Gardener very handsomely."

XX

LAST WILL, FINAL WALKS, CLOSING PRAYERS

L ike Versailles, Saint-Roch was permanently under construction.

The church at 286 rue Saint-Honoré was forever being expanded, altered, almost abandoned for lack of funding, suddenly restored to great activity, enlarged, beautified . . .

The story of this church starts at the beginning of the sixteenth century, with a chapel soon given the name of Saint-Roch, in tribute to a rich man of Montpellier who lived in the late Middle Ages. He had given all his worldly goods to the poor so he could devote himself to victims of the plague. Stricken in his turn, abandoned by one and all, save only a dog who brought him food each day, he had 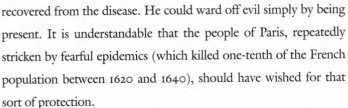 recovered from the disease. He could ward off evil simply by being present. It is understandable that the people of Paris, repeatedly stricken by fearful epidemics (which killed one-tenth of the French population between 1620 and 1640), should have wished for that sort of protection.

Saint-Roch deserved better than a mere chapel. In 1653, Louis

XIV laid the first stone for a new church that would end up almost as big as Notre-Dame (135 yards long). The architect was Jacques Lemercier, to whom we owe the Palais-Cardinal (later Palais-Royal) and part of the Louvre.

Money ran short; construction dragged on and would not be finished until 1740. Le Nôtre would not live to see his church progress beyond a roofing of wood planks. Neither the discomfort this occasioned, nor drafts of air, deflected him from his purpose: he wanted to be buried in Saint-Roch. Pierre Corneille had got there ahead of him, and Diderot would come later, as would many others: two admirals, a maréchal of France, a daughter of Louise de La Vallière, any number of sculptors, the abbé de l'Epée (inventor of deaf-mute language), Baron d'Holbach, Marie-Thérèse Geoffrin, hostess of the celebrated literary salon, and more. A kind of vogue had sprung up as soon as the place was opened and continuing until the Revolution, Saint-Roch was the place of choice for your eternal rest. It is a safe conjecture that this snobbish funerary fashion did not motivate Le Nôtre. Saint-Roch was simply his neighborhood church. His life as a Christian had started with being baptized there, and that was where it would end.

Le Nôtre was not Ulysses. He had no need to come home, for he had never left. He had been born at the Tuileries and knew he would die there. Italy was his only foreign journey and not a true journey at that, since every famous building he encountered, every painting he stopped to look at, had already been firmly rooted in his heart and mind since adolescence. His only trip to the farther reaches of

France had been—at the king's invitation—a visit to the siege of Valenciennes. It was a short stay, marked by surprise at finding himself in this strange company: military men and ladies of court, the latter applauding the exploits of the former, as though they were all at a theater together. Poliorcetics, the art of taking and defending fortified towns, was enjoyed as though it were an opera combined with an outing to the country: we all picnic on the grass and spend the night under canvas . . .

Aside from these two forays, no travels to distant parts. No one was less of an explorer than he. He was a walker, not a traveler. He walked; he walked endlessly, but without ever going away. He criss-crossed a garden of his creating, like Robinson Crusoe inspecting his island. And then he would go over to some other garden, some other island. Look at the map: Chantilly, Vaux, Sceaux, Versailles, Saint-Germain . . . The north and east, the south and west. As Vauban had ringed France, so Le Nôtre put a belt around Paris. *His* fortifications were parks. And they, too, served as protection. Not from hostile armies, but from the turmoils of life and the disorder of nature. Chantilly, Vaux, Sceaux, Versailles, Saint-Germain; with those strongholds of civilization securely anchored in the heart of Île-de-France, Le Nôtre could go back to his home and there await the end.

What are you supposed to do when for years you did so much and suddenly there is nothing more to be done? How are you supposed to lead your life, when a noisy crowd used to dog your every step, attentive to your every gesture, swallowing your least utterance as though from oracle issued, and now silence and solitude surround you instead? The retirement of professional people remains a mystery. Does the energy that has ceased to serve turn to boredom, then become transmuted into mental anguish? Or does peace of mind prevail, a mixture of proud satisfaction stemming from the job you have done and deep weariness stemming from the toll it has taken? Of course, everything depends on the individual and the moment. Nothing is permanent, moods least of all. From one hour to the next, tranquillity can turn to fright. No one will ever truly know what Le Nôtre's last years were like; no one will know whether, behind the face he put on (composure and *bonhomie*), he was assailed by terrors of one kind or another, by grudges and feelings of bitterness.

The facts we know for certain boil down to three: he reckoned, he walked, and he prayed.

* *
*

His legal testament was his last opus.

Drawing up a will is an engrossing business when you have property and money. Money and property that mean a great deal to you, especially since they didn't come easily, clients of highest rank being by no means the quickest to pay their bills. That remark applied especially to the state, crippled with debt, its coffers exhausted from the concurrent demands of war abroad and munificence at home.

Monsieur de Pontchartrain was comptroller-general of finance and owner of a park, designed of course by Le Nôtre, who sent him this sly love note:

You have been so good, My Lord, as to accept the plans for Pontchartrain, which you found to be quite well executed, and you have shewn that you were pleased with them. I used many pen-strokes, and drew a great number of different lines; all I ask of you in return is just one stroke of the pen, executed with your lovely white hand and including all the whirls and swirls needed for authorization to pay three thousand livres which it has pleased the King to give me every year, as a gratuity for services rendered by me to buildings in the year 1694, now ended. This, My Lord, you have promised your most humble and obedient servant. —Le Nostre.

Two years later he followed it up with an equally charming reminder:

My Lord, friends are friends; I have friends who shower me with flattering speeches: a crowned head, a principality, cardinals, an archbishop, a chancellor, a chief justice, an intendant of finances and the treasurer of a Savings Bank. But, sad to say, the only good and true friend is you, My Lord, the one friend who can make sure I am given and paid five thousand, two hundred and

eighty livres. You could not find better employ-
ment for the illustrious name of Pontchartrain
and Phélypeaux than on behalf of your most
humble and obedient servant.

This smiling obstinacy (combined with immense labors) bore
fruit. Le Nôtre's gifts to the king had barely made a dent in his collection. There were two hundred and fifty paintings, innumerable
prints and drawings (Raphael, Rembrandt, Rubens, Van Dyck ...),
twelve tapestries, statues, precious medallions, jewels, an overabun-
dance of silver plate. The inventory, which is extremely detailed, also
mentions pieces of Chinese porcelain and a few incongruous items
of the type that today would be called kitsch: a bagpipe, for instance,
hollowed out of a coconut dressed up in embroidery work and set
off with silver gilt; a little enclave of bad taste, delectable departures
from that elegant, orderly world (and existence).

His holdings in real estate (various houses in Paris and
Versailles) were easier to enumerate. As were the securities producing an annual income of eighteen thousand livres. Lastly, cash as-
sets: fifty-two thousand livres.

Le Nôtre finished listing his worldly goods and sat up straight.
Here was a life that had something to show besides the body of
artistic work. He called his wife to him, and arm in arm they set off
at their own pace, to go and complete the formalities:

He being thanks to God in perfect health, able to

come and go in the city as his own affairs may require, and having betaken himself to the house of Clément, one of the undersigned notaries, for the express purpose . . . etc.

Although the legatee's identity came as no surprise, the will did include a charmingly candid explanation:

Declaring that it has been the aforesaid lady, his spouse, who, by her good management and economy has seen to the preservation of such wealth as they have, whereas he, the testator, has always tended to lay out moneys for his workroom or collection with no thought for preserving wealth but rather honor and reputation, etc."[24]

Aside from her name being mentioned the day they were married, this is the only remaining trace of dame Le Nôtre. She was probably one of those household divinities whose powers operate in secrecy and anonymity. They quietly hold the reins that guide the conjugal home. They do not resist their husband's dreams and follies, but learn how to deduct at source the tithe that makes life comfortable and gives the family something to fall back on.

Having duly signed, they went home on foot, as they had come. Which shows that Walking had not abandoned Le Nôtre, despite his eighty-seven years. Walking was his friend. Walking was his ally, on an equal basis with Seeing. How can a man really look unless he walks? How can a man really garden unless he looks and walks? Perspective; it may be a creature of the eye, but only Walking can breathe life into it.

The next day and on subsequent days, right up to the end, the walks continued. When they saw him him go by, visitors to the Tuileries, or young men toiling with spades in the parterres, would point and murmur: Le Nôtre, that's Le Nôtre. They thought he was all by himself, fame notwithstanding; just the outline of a little old man slowly making his way along the allées. What they failed to grasp was that he had two companions, Walking and Seeing, two close friends that had been with him since he was a child and still regaled him with endless wonders. I suspect that somewhere around the year 1698 or 1699, God summoned Old Age and spoke these words that brooked no arguments: you will spare Le Nôtre the cruelties you customarily inflict, blindness, paralysis, and the like. Old Age cursed and swore, but had to submit. No doubt he got his revenge by visiting upon some other unfortunate human the major infirmities he had meant for the king's friend.

* * *

Profuse in recording whatever concerned his possessions, about his work Le Nôtre remained silent to the last. All his fellow gardeners, before departing this world, confided to paper their drawings, their ideas and the secrets of their art. Boyceau de La Barauderie and his

Traité du jardinage selon les raisons de la nature et de l'art, Claude Mollet (*Théâtre des plans et jardinages*), Claude's son André (*Le Jardin de plaisir*), La Quintinie with his *Instructions pour les jardins fruitiers et potagers* (Instructions for fruit and vegetable gardens) . . . Nothing of that sort in Le Nôtre's case. No journal, no memoirs. Not even the bother of collecting a few papers in one place to serve as an archive. He committed his works to the vagaries of time, to survive on their own, or not. Let others, should they so desire, study the works and infer underlying principles or systems.

Antoine-Joseph Dézallier d'Argenville, born in 1680, was an art lover, a natural science enthusiast specializing in seashells, and, young though he was, already a renowned collector of fossils . . . As he neared his thirtieth year, he developed a passion for plants and went walking at Versailles, Marly, and Chantilly, notebook in hand and faculties fully alert. His book, *La Théorie et la pratique du jardinage*, deals successively with each of the parts or places that make up a garden. Just to read the chapter titles is an enchanting exercise: "On Paths, Side-Paths, and Hedges"; "On Porticos, Bowers, and Trellised Arbors." Admirable in its use of language, his *Théorie* teaches us "the rules that must be followed." It was first published in 1709, then went through several editions, and was studied everywhere. It kept Le Nôtre's art alive throughout Europe until the end of the eighteenth century.

* * *

His very last walks took him down the paths of memory. Over and over, in his mind's eye, he inspected his gardens of the past, marveling at the diverse beauty he had brought into being. Take, by way of illustration, this letter of July 1698, addressed to the count of Portland and rediscovered by Ernest de Ganay. The Englishman had visited Chantilly; Le Nôtre had been unable to go with him and is lamenting the fact (flavorsome spellings have been retained):

> Milor and Monseigneur,
>
> . . . Had but my grete youthful spirit let me go, I know the pleasure I would have givn his Highness and I would have had the honor of pointing out to you the most beautiful parts and hearing you confess that it is a fine natural spectacle to see a river fall with an astonishing drop and forms the entrance to an endless canal. You must not ask where the water of that canal comes from. Forgive me, I could get carried away about many things [at Chantilly], since I was the one who had the planning of it down to the last avenue, and when you are come out of the forest, go in onto the terrace, which may easily be espied on the edge of the grand Stairway. If I am carried away it is because I am telling all this to the person I have found who has the best taste; there be very few

who understand the beauty that is in gardens or
works of architecture. Do not think, Milor, that I
flatter you; you are not taken in by vaine praises.

Even though he had not walked its grounds for ten years and
more, every detail of that beloved place was etched in his mind and
made him happy. The end of his letter rings out like an appeal: "Do
not forget the many gardens you have seen in France, Versailles,
Fontainebleau, Vaux-le-Vicomte and the Tuileries, and specially
Chantilly."

He must have envied architects, because they work in stone, less
soluble in time than the neatness of pathways. He knew, who better,
the impermanence of gardens. Three untended months in the
spring, and the work of thirty years can vanish under brambles and
brushwood.

Concern about the life eternal, as the end draws near, is more
readily understandable in a gardener than in some other person. For
his very last walks, the place he preferred to go was Saint-Roch.
There, meticulous in this as in all things, he ordered his final abode,
a grave dug in Saint-André Chapel. No armorial bearings, but a bust
commissioned from Coysevox. The epitaph was to be graven on
black marble and fastened to the first pillar:

To the glory of God
Here lies the body of André Le Nostre,
Chevalier of the Order of Saint-Michel,

Member of the Royal Council, general superintendent of
His Majesty's buildings, crafts, and
manufactories of France, and appointed
to develop the gardens of Versailles
and other royal
residences.

The strength and scope of his genius
made him so outstanding in the art of gardening
that he may be considered as having
invented
the chief beauties of that art and brought
all the others to their ultimate degree of perfection.
In one sense, the excellence of his created works
was a response to the greatness
and magnificence of the Monarch whom he served
and who
lavished upon him marks of Royal favor.
France was not the sole beneficiary
of his talents. All the princes of Europe
sought his apprentices.
He had no rival that could be compared
to him.
He was born in the year 1613 and died in the month of
September, in the year 1700.

Did he compose the epitaph himself and leave destiny to inscribe the final date but only that? I wouldn't be surprised. His was a quiet kind of pride, but quiet does not mean small.

The funeral eulogies, too, were ready in advance. He knew that everyone liked him, even Saint-Simon the grump, and that his passing would be mourned by all, first and foremost by the king.

Come, now, nothing had been overlooked; it was time to die.

15 September 1700. Clocks struck 4:00 A.M. Le Nôtre had gone. He was now part of the heavens, those same heavens that, with mirroring waters and open perspectives, he had welcomed so freely into his gardens.

The rest, as you know, is mystery.

1. For a walk through the park in its early days, you could ask no better companion than Geneviève Bresc-Bautier and Denis Caget in collaboration with Emmanuel Jacquin, *Jardins du Carrousel et des Tuileries* (Paris: Réunion des musées nationaux, 1996).

2. Philippe Comar, *La Perspective en jeu* (Paris: Gallimard, 1992).

3. Thierry Mariage, *L'Univers de Le Nostre* (Brussels: Pierre Mardaga, 1990).

4. Comar, *La Perspective en jeu*.

5. Mariage, *L'Univers de Le Nostre*.

6. Louis XIII quoted by Mariage, *L'Univers de Le Nostre*.

7. Allen S. Weiss, *Miroirs de l'infini. Le jardin à la française et la métaphysique au XVIIe siècle* (Paris: Le Seuil, 1992).

8. Jean-Christian Petitfils, *Louis XIV* (Paris: Perrin, 1995).

9. José Cabanis, *Saint-Simon l'admirable* (Paris: Gallimard, 1974).

10. Jean-Christian Petitfils, *Louis XIV*.

11. Philippe Beaussant, *Versailles, Opéra* (Paris: Gallimard, 1981); and Philippe Beaussant, *Louis XIV artiste* (Paris: Payot, 1999).

12. Jean-Marie Apostolidès, *Le Roi-machine* (Paris: Éditions de Minuit, 1981).

13. Pierre de Nolhac, *Les Jardins de Versailles* (Paris, 1906); Ernest de Ganay, *André Le Nôtre* (Paris, 1962).

14. L. A. Barbet, *Les Grands Eaux de Versailles* (Paris, 1907).

15. Barbet, *Les Grandes Eaux de Versailles*.

16. Alfred Mousset, *Les Francine* (Paris, 1930).

17. Michel Corajoud, Jacques Coulon, and Marie-Hélène Loze, *Versailles: lecture d'un jardin* (Paris, 1982).

18. de Ganay, *André Le Nôtre;* Bernard Jeannel, *Le Nôtre* (Paris: Hazan, 1985).

19. Jeannel, *Le Nôtre*.

20. Mariage, *L'Univers de Le Nostre*.

21. de Ganay, *André Le Nôtre*.

22. Marc Fumaroli's indispensable study *Le Poète et le Roi* (Paris: De Fallois, 1997), makes fascinating reading.

23. Quoted by Jean-Michel Delacomptée, *Racine en majesté* (Paris: Flammarion, 1999).

24. de Ganay, *André Le Nôtre*.

LIST OF ILLUSTRATIONS

All illustrations (except Bretez map details) reprinted from *The French
Garden 1500–1800* by William Howard Adams (Braziller, 1979)

ACKNOWLEDGMENTS/BIBLIOGRAPHY

Any book is made up of other books; in the writing of this one, I combed more pages than I roamed garden paths. I owe these guides more than gratitude; I owe them some sort of friendship. They made me a gift of our Golden Age. Despite Racine, despite Molière and La Fontaine, despite forty years of weekly walks along the Grand Canal, my mental picture of the seventeenth century, based on what I remembered from school, was only a caricature: a marble monument locked in by religion, paralyzed by etiquette, and crushed by boredom. The facts are quite otherwise: it was a time of passionate feeling—passion in the pursuit of reason as in the pursuit of pleasures, a passion for the grandiose but also for minutiae.

So, to these special companions, thanks!

On the General History of Gardens

Baridon, Michel. *Les Jardins.* Paris: Robert Laffont, 1998.

Conan, Michel. *Dictionnaire historique de l'art des jardins.* Paris, 1955.

A Few Bibles

Androuet Du Cerceau, Jacques. *Les Plus Excellents Bâtiments de France.* 1576.

Boyceau de La Barauderie, Jacques. *Traité du jardinage selon les raisons de la nature et de l'art* (Treatise on gardening following the dictates of nature and art). 1638.

de Caus, Salomon. *La Perspective avec la raison des ombres et des miroirs* (Perspective, along with the ratios of shadows and mirrors). 1612.

——. *Hortus Palatinus.* 1620.

Dézallier d'Argenville, Antoine-Joseph. *La Théorie et la pratique du jardinage.* 1709.

Mollet, Claude. *Théâtre des plans et jardinages* (Manual of garden plans and procedures). Posthumous, 1652.

de Serres, Olivier. *Théâtre d'agriculture et mesnage des champs.* 1600.

On Le Nôtre

Two irreplaceable syntheses:

de Nolhac, Pierre. *Les Jardins de Versailles.* Paris, 1906.

de Ganay, Ernest. *André Le Nôtre.* Paris, 1962.

And two summary accounts by architects, insight and intelligence in capsule form:

Jeannel, Bernard. *Le Nôtre.* Paris: Hazan, 1985.

Mariage, Thierry. *L'Univers de Le Nostre.* Brussels: Pierre Mardaga, 1990

On the Science and Technology of the Time

Barbet, L. A. *Les Grandes Eaux de Versailles* (The fountains at Versailles). Paris, 1907. An engineer describes in painstaking detail the follies of a monarch whose chief preoccupation was how to satisfy the fountains.

Comar, Philippe. *La Perspective en jeu* (Perspective at work). Découvertes. Paris: Gallimard, 1992. A guided tour of the eye, its aspirations, and its tricks, in 120 lucid pages.

Gille, Bertrand. *Les Ingénieurs de la Renaissance.* Paris, 1964.

Panofsky, Erwin. *La Perspective comme forme symbolique.* Paris, 1975.

Weiss, Allen S. *Miroirs de l'infini. Le jardin à la française et la métaphysique au XVIIe siècle.* Paris: Le Seuil, 1992. Exemplar of the philosophical stroll. Especially stimulating for Weiss's reading of Vaux.

On Louis XIV and Versailles

Apostolidès, Jean-Marie. *Le Roi-machine.* Paris: Éditions de Minuit, 1981.

Astier, Hubert. *Versailles, parc et château.* Paris: Éditions du huitième jour, 2000.

Beaussant, Philippe. *Versailles, Opéra.* Paris: Gallimard, 1981.

———. *Louis XIV artiste.* Paris: Payot, 1999.

Beaussant, Philippe, with the collaboration of Patricia Bouchenot-Déchin. *Les Plaisirs de Versailles: Théâtre et musique.* Paris: Fayard, 1996.

Cabanis, José. *Saint-Simon l'admirable*. Paris: Gallimard, 1974.

Déon, Michel. *Louis XIV par lui-même*. Paris, 1991.

Fumaroli, Marc. *Le Poète et le Roi*. Paris: De Fallois, 1997.

Lablaude, Pierre-André, and Jean-Pierre Babelon. *Les Jardins de Versailles*. Paris: Scala, 1995.

Mariage, Thierry. *Trianon, l'autre côté du rivage*. Paris: Éditions du huitième jour, 2000.

Petitfils, Jean-Christian. *Louis XIV*. Paris: Perrin, 1995.

Voltaire. *Le Siècle de Louis XIV*. La Pléiade. Paris: Gallimard, 1971.

On the Tuileries

Bresc-Bautier, Geneviève, and Denis Caget, with the collaboration of Emmanuel Jacquin. *Jardins du Carrousel et des Tuileries* (The Carrousel and Tuileries Gardens). Paris: Réunion des musées nationaux, 1996. Five centuries of history, a model of lively erudition.

On the Seventeenth Century

Bluche, François, ed. *Dictionnaire du Grand Siècle*. Paris: Fayard, 1990. A great opus with 248 contributors, 2,413 articles, 2,413 doors to the Golden Age; open the ones that tempt you.

Mandrou, Robert. *La France aux XVIIe et XVIIIe siècles*. Paris, 1971 and Paul Morand's first-rate study *Fouquet ou le Soleil offusqué*. Paris: Gallimard, 1961.

And La Fontaine and Saint-Simon and Racine and Molière and Cardinal de Retz and Tallement des Réaux and Charles Perrault (*Les Mémoires de ma vie*).

A Few Other Writers to Keep You Company on Your Walks

Bachelard, Gaston. *L'Eau et les Rêves*. Paris: José Corti, 1942.

Corajoud, Michel, Jacques Coulon, and Marie-Hélène Loze. *Versailles: lecture d'un jardin* (A reading of the garden at Versailles). Paris, 1982.

Delacomptée, Jean-Michel. *Racine en majesté*. Paris: Flammarion, 1999.

Fleury, Michel, ed., with the collaboration of Guy-Michel Leproun and François Monnier. *Almanach de Paris*. Paris, 1990.

France, Anatole. *Vaux-le-Vicomte*. Paris, 1933.

Guiffrey, Jules. *André Le Nôtre*. Paris, 1912.

Mousset, Alfred. *Les Francine*. Paris, 1930.

Pechère, René. *Grammaire des jardins*. Brussels, 1995.

Pérouse de Montclos, Jean-Marie. *Vaux-le-Vicomte*. Paris, 1997.

Vérin, Hélène. *La Gloire des ingénieurs*. Paris: Albin Michel, 1993.

And my thanks to Jean-Baptiste Cuisinier, Director of the École nationale supérieure du paysage, who helped me develop a taste for mathematical happiness.

BY ÉRIK ORSENNA

Loyola's Blues, Paris, Éditions du Seuil, 1974; republished "Points-Seuil," 1989.

La Vie comme à Lausanne, Paris, Éditions du Seuil, 1977; republished "Points-Seuil," 1989.

Une comédie francaise, Paris, Éditions du Seuil, 1980; republished "Points-Seuil," 1981.

Villes d'eaux, Paris, Ramsay, 1981 (in collaboration with Jean-Marc Terrasse).

L'Exposition coloniale, Paris, Éditions du Seuil, 1988; republished "Points-Seuil," 1995.

Besoin d'Afrique, Paris, Fayard, 1992 (in collaboration with Éric Fottorino and Christophe Guillemin); republished LGF, 1994.

Grand Amour, Paris, Éditions du Seuil, 1993; republished "Points-Seuil," 1995.

Rochefort et la Corderie royale (photographs by Eddie Kuligowsski), Paris, CNMHS, 1995.

Histoire du monde en neuf guitares, Paris, Fayard, 1996 (with accompaniment by Thierry Arnoult).

Mésaventure du paradis: mélodie cubaine (photographs by Bernard Matussière), Paris, Éditions du Seuil, 1996.

Deux Étés, Paris, Fayard, 1997.

Longtemps, Paris, Fayard, 1998.